A taste of Functional Programming in Scala

Malay Mandal

About the book

This book is -
not a book of fiction
not intended to be a primary textbook for learning Scala
nor a complete reference on functional programming

However it is an attempt at presentation of some concepts of functional programming in an easily understandable manner. It also presents a lot of actual coding [solutions to problems presented or demonstrative code] which may be adopted (with proper modifications) to some day to day FP tasks

Intended audience : Programmers who knows Java well, and may be having some preliminary knowledge of Scala, but want to learn some Functional Programming concepts the easy way.

...

Sometimes easier explanation of an involved technical matter may require more space (sometimes considerably more), than a condensed technical treatise. Think of a zipped and unzipped file. Hence probably a reference book on the subject of Functional Programming will cover more material, in the same number of pages. However I hope the advantage you enjoy here - is much easier and possibly enjoyable reading, and learning what you learn, in a way, that you can apply easily, but do not forget so easily.

Many of the things present in the book are more in the mode of explanation / illustration (in my own way) rather than a verbatim definition.

What you are getting into

(And by this I do not mean Functional Programming, but this book.)

If you have full access to the printed form of the book, you can flip through pages, and check a paragraph here and one there, to satisfy your curiosity as to what you are getting into. In some form of soft publication also, at least some pages are visible. However I thought it would be appropriate to give you a hint of what you are getting into.

Here are two excerpts from parts of the book.
The first one involves a piece of code and corresponding explanation.

def canMake(dish: String): Boolean =

recipes.get(dish).map(_.map(pantry.get(_))).map(sequence(_)).flatten.map(_ => true).getOrElse(false)

In the way of explanation -
recipes.get(dish) will produce an Option with a List of ingredients (Strings) wrapped in Some, for a valid dish, or None if an invalid dish was enquired. The first map on that - gets the List inside (for valid recipes), and the second map is on that List (of Strings). The mapping on ingredients List looks through the pantry for each required ingredients, and produces an ingredient (String) wrapped in Some or None (for each one of them), and hence it finally produces a list of Options. The outer map (first map) makes it an Option (of List of Options) so another map is needed to get out the List of Options form that Option of List of Options. Which is then passed through the sequence function to produce an Option of List (either a List of ingredients wrapped in Some if all ingredients are available, or None). But the sequence itself is occurring within a map of Option. So the overall result of the map will be Option of Option of List, and hence a flatten is needed to

reduce one level of optioning to an Option of List. A map on that, is simply checking if a List exists (which means all ingredients are available) in which case it returns true. Otherwise, if a list does not exist inside the option, it may either mean, the name of dish was invalid so None was available from recipes Map, or that all the ingredients were not available in the pantry. In either case it is a false. The dish is not possible to be prepared.

The other, is part of a discussion on programming style.

In matters of explanation and illustration, sometimes a comparison helps. Sometimes a contrast proves to be a better tool. (Eventually at times, a combination of comparison and contrast is called into action).

In order to understand what a programming style is, let's look at what other programming styles we may be already familiar with. Perhaps the first one is 'procedural programming style' or 'imperative style' (such as followed in C language). The next one may be 'object oriented programming style' (such as followed in Java).

A programming style, is a way of organizing a program, and a way of expressing the computation that needs to be done.

In procedural style, it is all sequential. Program is expressed largely as a series of commands (statements) [the overall path of flow - often structured with control statements such as if and for]. In object oriented style, things are organized in objects (encapsulated data, and methods that can perform operations on the data – [shaped into templates through classes, that all object of the type would follow]). 'Objects rather than actions and data rather than logic' somewhat being the core of the structural modularization. The overall program structure builds largely upon the interaction of objects.

This would hopefully give you a taste of the book (which itself is on taste of FP, of course). If you do not like much of what is said here (and more importantly how it is said), you are possibly not going to like the book.

Enough said - let's focus on who you should be.

Who you should be

This is again not an attempt to create or check a personality profile, but rather to describe the technical profile of a target reader, who could (hopefully) benefit from the book.

In order to make good use of the book, you would need to be a programmer (whether professional or occasional), with some basic coding skill in Scala. (This is not a textbook for learning Scala language among other things). If you have some basic and amorphous idea about functional programming, that does not hurt. However someone completely new to functional programming also should (hopefully) be able to get somewhere with the book. In fact an occasional Scala programmer, with little or no knowledge of functional programming would, in my view, be ideally positioned to use the book.

What not to expect

This book is not a complete treatise on functional programming. In fact as the name suggests, it is meant to give you a taste of functional programming. Some concepts and a few aspects are discussed in some detail, that should hopefully get you going with some basic application of functional programming even in day to day professional programming. And can be leveraged as a starting point for further learning. But if you wish to be an expert in functional programming, this book is do not present the sufficient condition.

What could be (hopefully) expected

Not all is lost though. This book do have some good points in it's favour -

It is small in size (and because of that would possibly not be too expensive also). But small size (especially for a book) has another advantage. You can finish it quicker (although in this regard complexity of subject and fluidity of language weighs in too), and hopefully learn ,what you were to learn from it, quicker.

It has been (hopefully) presented in a rather simple to understand way. While there are good book(s) of functional programming in Scala, I have not come across any, which is easy to follow [in fact anything that comes close to it]. (It is possible that I didn't look hard enough). That is one of the motivations for my writing the book the way I did. A functional programming (in Scala) book, that you can read easily, is possibly not commonplace.

This book has a few solutions discussed, which (at least in parts) could be adopted - either readily or with little modifications, for some common day to day Scala scripting needs.

(I may think of writing a sequel for the book, covering some other aspects of functional programming [especially if this book appears to be received well])

Notes

- This book often made use of expressions such as - Let's discuss <some topic>. The reader was not physically present with me, however I found this linguistic style a good way of introducing topics, or otherwise maintaining the flow of expression.

- The code presented in this book is generally tested on Scala 2.11.8

- All the (coding) problems presented in the book are solved in the book itself (solution code fully contained in the book). So you won't need to download any extra code from elsewhere.

Table of Contents

The story begins 1

  A taste of conciseness 1

  Functional Programming : what why and how 9

  What is Functional Programming...............................12

  What is a computer ? 13

  Putting two and two together.................................15

  Setting up the shop 18

    Download 18

    For Windows 18

    For Mac..19

  And saying Hello 20

  REPL 20

Functional functions 22

  Higher Order Functions 23

    Functions as variables 23

    Function types 24

    Function as parameters to functions 26

    Anonymous Functions......................................27

    Functions within functions 29

    Functions as return values 31

    Storing functions in data structures.....................32

  Referential Transparency.....................................35

    Definition? 35

    Referential 36

    Transparency 38

    Explanation (of definition) 40

  Why RT is necessary?...41

    'piece reliability' 43

    memoization..45

    order of execution.......................................45

    lazy evaluation..46

    and what is program 46

  In the wilderness 46

  Pure functions 48

Immutability 49
Types, functions, and classes – a little more Scala 51
The importance of typing 52
Scala types in general 53
Non-primitive types 53
Type inference 53
Immutability of value 54
Type aliasing 55
Placeholder syntax...56
Polymorphic functions 57
Type Constructors 58
Polymorphic functions and type constructors 59
Classes 60
Tuples 63
Few functional tricks 65
Default parameters...65
Multiple parameter set......................................65
Implicit parameters...66
by-name parameters 67
Lazy and eager evaluation of functions 71
def, val and lazy val.......................................71
Derived functions 72
Tupled 73
Partially applied functions 73
Currying 74
Uncurrying 78
Composition of functions 78
Traits 79
Recursive functions...82
The Factorial 83
Crux of recursion stepping....................................86
Tail recursion 95
Binary search algorithm 99
Pattern matching in Scala 109
Pattern matching with cases...................................109
Value match 110

Expression match 112
Type match 113
Extracting tokens 114
Match on cons operator.............................118
Match for a Map 120
Case classes and pattern matching 121
Covariance and Contravariance....................128
Assignment compatibility vs variance 129
Assignment compatibility 129
covariance 130
covariance in action : delivering machines 132
contravariance...135
contravariance in action : for a few more dollars 136
Invariant...138
Liskov substitution principle in context ...139
The Icon Rule..140
In defence of variance...........................141
Functional transformations 144
What is data structure ? 145
Algebraic Data Types 146
data structures vs collections 149
Importance of collective data 150
List - a functional data structure...............151
What is List...151
Why List 152
Construction of List 154
Transformations on List 156
map 157
filter 161
Anatomy of map and filter.....................163
fold..167
fold and tail recursion 170
foldLeft examples....................................172
Raising and lowering to the level............173
flatten..173
flatMap..174

Following the types..176
Transformations on List (continued...)....................177
   Anatomy of foldLeft and flatMap 180
   more predicate based transformations..........182
   takeWhile and dropWhile 182
   partition 183
   Lazy traversal..184
   zip 187
   zipWithIndex..188
   grouping 188
   reduce..190
  map-reduce 190
Functional transformation – a demonstration.........204
Exception handling – functional way 215
  Option 218
   Packing and unpacking..............................221
   map and filter 226
   Anatomy of map and filter 227
   flatMap and fold......................................228
  'Optionifying' functions...............................235
  List and Option 236
   Flattening List of Options.........................236
   Sequence 237
   example – ingredients and recipes 240
   example – bonus report 244

The story begins

Sometimes avoiding shortcuts make the journey more enjoyable.

A taste of conciseness

Functional Programming in general and Functional Programming in Scala in particular, has it's advantages. One of the advantages – which is partly owed to Functional Programming and partly to Scala as a language – is, it makes the code quiet concise. A little demonstration follows.

...

Suppose, you are employed by a bank, and you are to develop a back end functionality for an ATM. The task to be accomplished is described as -

Given a transaction file which lists transactions on multiple accounts, (in a certain format)

When a function is run, with an account number, and an amount (to be withdrawn) as argument

Then

If the account is non existent in the transaction file, the function returns a string indicating an invalid account.

If the account exists, but does not have enough balance left to withdraw the amount indicated, then the program returns a string indicating not enough balance.

If the account exists and the balance is sufficient for the withdrawal, the program returns a string indicating successful withdrawal and final balance.

(The balance at any stage is calculated by summing up all the transaction amounts till that point)

The contents of the transaction file is given below. There is no header, and the columns indicate account number, date, description and amount. It shows transactions from three accounts (but note that, it is possible to have transactions from more accounts in the file, so the program should not validate accounts based on hardcoded account numbers).

tran.txt :

101,01-01-2016,opening balance,200.00

102,01-01-2016,opening balance,50.00

103,01-01-2016,opening balance,100.00

101,02-01-2016,purchase from ebay,-132.00

102,02-01-2016,gift from friend,65.00

103,02-01-2016,purchase from flipkart,-92.00

102,03-01-2016,withdrawal from atm,-80.00

101,03-01-2016,refund of ticket,12.00

101,03-01-2016,purchase from Amazon,-60.00

102,03-01-2016,cash deposit,20.00

103,03-01-2016,cheque deposit,32.00

103,03-01-2016,atm withdrawal,-20.00

102,04-01-2016,online purchase,-35.00

103,04-01-2016,cash deposit,50.00

102,04-01-2016,refund for goods,10.00

101,04-01-2016,royalty deposit,20.00

(the name of the transaction file is 'tran.txt'). Although in the transaction file, all the entries are Strings (comma separated), in the program the account numbers should be Int, and amounts Double. At this point do not consider exception handling (beyond what is forced by the language). Assume the file exists and all data rows have valid data.

...

I have written some Java and Scala code to solve the problem.

The Java code is as follows.

```java
package acct;

import java.io.BufferedReader;
import java.io.File;
import java.io.FileNotFoundException;
import java.io.FileReader;
import java.io.IOException;
import java.util.ArrayList;
import java.util.HashSet;
import java.util.List;
import java.util.Set;

public class Acct {

    public static void main(String[] args) {
        System.out.println("(104, 20) => " + atm(104, 20.0));
        System.out.println("(102, 50) => " + atm(102, 50.0));
        System.out.println("(103, 20) => " + atm(103, 20.0));
    }
}
```

```java
static String atm(int acct, Double amt) {
    Set<Integer> acctSet = new HashSet<>();

    for (Txn txn : txnLst()) {
        acctSet.add(txn.getAcct());
    }

    if (!acctSet.contains(acct)) {
        return "Not a valid account";
    } else {
        Double balance = acctBalance(acct) - amt;
        if (balance < 0) {
            return "Not enough balance";
        } else {
            return "Balance after withdrawal is " +
balance;
        }
    }
}

static Double acctBalance(int acctNo) {

    Double amt = 0.0;

    for (Txn txn : txnLst()) {
        if (txn.getAcct() == acctNo)
```

```
                    amt += txn.getAmt();
        }


        return amt;

    }


    static List<Txn> txnLst() {
        List<Txn> txnList = new ArrayList<>();
        try {
            BufferedReader acct = new
BufferedReader(new FileReader(new File("tran.txt")));
            String line = "";
            try {
                while((line = acct.readLine())
!= null) {
                    String[] arr =
line.split(",");

                    Txn txn = new
Txn(arr[0], arr[3]);

                    txnList.add(txn);
                }
                acct.close();
            } catch (IOException e) {
                e.printStackTrace();
            }
        } catch (FileNotFoundException e) {
            e.printStackTrace();
        }
```

```
        return txnList;
    }
}


class Txn {

    private int acct;
    private Double amt;

    public Txn(String acctStr, String amtStr) {
        this.acct = Integer.parseInt(acctStr);
        this.amt = Double.parseDouble(amtStr);
    }

    public int getAcct() {
        return acct;
    }

    public Double getAmt() {
        return amt;
    }
}
```

Note that there are some exception handling, but they are checked exceptions, somewhat forced by the language in this scenario.

Upon running the code, it provides all three cases of result, for three different function calls. And the results are -

(104, 20) => Not a valid account

(102, 50) => Not enough balance

(103, 20) => Balance after withdrawal is 50.0

For the benefit of judgement, for the given transaction file (as it stands, before the function run), the net balance of the accounts are as follows -

101 => 40.00

102 => 30.00

103 => 70.00

...

The Scala code, which produces the same result, is -

```
package acct


import scala.io.Source


object Acct {
  def main(args: Array[String]) = {
    println("(104, 20) => " + atm(104, 20))
    println("(102, 50) => " + atm(102, 50))
    println("(103, 20) => " + atm(103, 20))
  }


  def txnLst = for ( line <- Source.fromFile("tran.txt").getLines )
    yield(line.split(",") match { case Array(a,b,c,d) => (a.toInt,
d.toDouble)})


  def atm(acct: Int, amt: Double): String = {
```

```scala
if (!txnLst.map (_._1).toSet.contains(acct))
    "Not a valid account"
else {
    val balance = txnLst.filter(_._1 == acct).map(_._2).sum - amt
    if (balance < 0)
        "Not enough balance"
    else
        "Balance after withdrawal is " + balance
  }
 }

}
```

Does not require much imagination to guess, that the code is much smaller than it's Java counterpart.

How small ?

Line, word and character count goes as -

```
91    236    1887 Acct.java
26    94     709 Acct.scala
```

In terms of character count, (which is perhaps most reliable judge of relative size, of the three), the Scala code is less than 40% in volume compared to the Java counterpart.

If you consider that *main* function is the driving code (not the core part of processing) and leave that aside from size comparison (from both Java and Scala code). And if you also leave aside String literals such as "Not a valid account" - the rest of code on Scala side could come down to about 1/3 of similar part of code in Java.

...

Note that lesser code volume would mean lesser number

of bugs in general, as they would be easier to spot.

...

Ironically, if I remember correctly, this conciseness of Scala and Functional Programming, is what attracted my attention to Scala in the first place. And although that is by no means the only advantage functional programming has to offer [and the argument about conciseness, for now, still involves Scala], it still continues to be a major point of attraction for me.

...

The point of conciseness, and related argument, was attempted as a stage introduction (in a manner of speaking) prior to the entry of the main performer (in this case the discussion in earnest on functional programming – which is the subject matter of the book). So let's push ahead towards the core.

Functional Programming : what why and how

Let me be upfront. This section isn't going to address all of these points in complete detail. In fact the whole book is largely about catering to that. In fact, if you come to think of it – this (i.e. to learn the *what, why and how of functional programming)*, would possibly be an underlying motivation for any book on functional programming, you decide to read. This section is more towards setting some headline answers, and getting you started thinking in the terms of *what, why and how of functional programming.*

What is Functional Programming is discussed in good detail, in a section, soon to follow. However why and how part is slightly less straightforward.

...

For why part, I do not see a way out other than philosophy. Why do you learn something, or practice something for that matter?

To make things simpler let's bring in an analogy. Why would someone want to learn or practice martial arts, like Karate or Jujitsu?

Now don't get me wrong, people sometimes do things for truly grotesque reasons. But I am not going there. What would be some of the usual reasons for someone, trying to learn martial arts.

Some of the reasons I can think of would be – self defence, physical fitness, being better in some other sports, may be even personal vendetta (against someone physically stronger), or trying to right some perceived wrongs.

But these are only some of the possible reasons. As someone explores the nuances of a particular discipline of martial arts, he may come up with perfectly reasonable, but quite innovative use of his skills.

Such is perhaps the case with in depth study in any field of learning, Functional Programming included. While there are some usual reasons, such as easy reasoning of computation, robustness (and with that horizontal scalability), better testability and taking advantage of structural algebra in processing, (many of which, hopefully, will become apparent, as you go on reading the book), as your learning an involvement deepens, you may find many more intriguing use of the style, tools and techniques that functional programming offers.

...

That brings us to the how part. Here too, the same analogy will be helpful. If you are to ask a great expert in martial arts – 'How to do Karate?' (Think of Mr. Miyagi in the movie 'The Karate Kid' if it helps), I am not sure, he will be able to answer you, in one or two sentences (And even if he does, I am pretty sure, that would be a very philosophical answer).

But if you come to think of it, in a martial arts class (as much as I know), they teach different types of kicking, punching, blocking, arm locking, techniques of falling to the ground which minimize the effect of impact, movements that are aimed at protecting vulnerable parts of your body, and so on. In other words, it teaches a set of tools, techniques (and possibly philosophies), that, properly practised may make you an expert in the field. [There may be other aspect to martial arts also, such as synchronizing your emotional state with your movements – but for the purpose of my analogy, I would like to focus on the more material essence of the teaching]

The answer to 'How to do functional programming?' too – is somewhat similar. The learning (in my view), consists in learning some specific style, tools, and techniques (and possibly philosophy), which, harmonized together in their right places, makes up the totality* of functional programming. [* although as more people explore the field, newer tools may be unveiled and added to the repertoire].

Such tools include - data structures and collections suited to functional programming needs, functional types, type variance, partial function application, abstraction of parallelism, functional state, functional testing, functional structures, stream processing and so on. Note that, since in this book that medium of functional programming is Scala, any tools and techniques discussed will naturally be based upon implementation of that tool or technique in Scala. However the basic principle is quiet often independent of the language.

...

Hopefully now you have a slightly better idea of what to expect from a functional programming book (or at least from this book in particular). Note that, this book being a book that is meant to provide some taste of it - would only discuss some of the topics, and not all.

What is Functional Programming

Short answer : It is a programming style.

Now if you feel like asking, 'What is programming style?' you will not be delving very far away from my expectation of your questioning (at least in terms of the first question).

...

In matters of explanation and illustration, sometimes a comparison helps. Sometimes a contrast proves to be a better tool. (Eventually at times, a combination of comparison and contrast is called into action).

In order to understand what a programming style is, let's look at what other programming styles we may be already familiar with. Perhaps the first one is 'procedural programming style' or 'imperative style' (such as followed in C language). The next one may be 'object oriented programming style' (such as followed in Java).

A programming style, is a way of organizing a program, and a way of expressing the computation that needs to be done.

In procedural style, it is all sequential. Program is expressed largely as a series of commands (statements) [the overall path of flow - often structured with control statements such as if and for]. In object oriented style, things are organized in objects (encapsulated data, and methods that can perform operations on the data – [shaped into templates through classes, that all object of the type would follow]). 'Objects rather than actions and data rather than logic' somewhat being the core of the structural modularization. The overall program structure builds largely upon the interaction of objects.

The key sentence here, as you might appreciate is - *A programming style, is a way of organizing a program, and a way of expressing the computation that needs to be done.* While this may serve as a (rather unofficial) definition of what a programming style is, this possibly does not go very far in explaining to a beginner, what it really means. [And this book is more about explanation and understanding, than about definitions]. Hence this point will be elaborated on, rather early, in the unfolding of the narrative.

...

You would be perfectly justified in asking a second question – 'Why do we need this programming style'? (this referring to FP). The answer to this question – in a way – is given throughout this book. That is, as you read this book, hopefully you will find many reasons why you would like to use Functional Programming.

What is a computer ?

And this can get very philosophical. A dictionary may define the word in a certain way. Perhaps referring to this as an electronic device, and something that is programmable. A subject in Computer Science may define it in a very different manner. But why do I start with this question here? Isn't it too elementary for a book which should be on programming?

Well, sometimes getting back to the basics, goes a long way to unravel something that may seem rather complicated (or even very complicated) on the outset. In detective serials (especially the ones involving murder), sometimes they talk about means, motive and opportunity. And sometimes, in absence of any one of them, the hero (or heroine) may not be convinced, that the suspect indeed is the killer, even though a good number of clues are pointing otherwise.

...

Without getting too philosophical, if we accept that *a computer is a programable device that computes* (which of course is a bespoke description for the purpose of my current discussion), we can extend the argument by proposing that a programme (which is essentially *a detailed instruction of that computation*) should *express the computation details (steps) in such a way – as to make it functionally accurate, efficient, well organized, and possibly to make it easy to understand and reason with.*

Already seems like, this is asking for a lot, isn't it ? Accurate – we can understand, it should be bug free. Efficient ? Eh! Did someone not say 'A computer can make as many mistakes in 20 seconds, as 20000 men would make in 20 years' (or something similar)? *Why do we need efficient programs, when we have efficient computers?* And on top of that some piece of code that is 'easy to understand and reason with'? What are you, a Martian? Do they not use iPhones on Mars?

Well, to start with, the four attributes (of program expression) that I talked about, namely -
- functional accuracy
- (proper) organization
- efficiency of execution and
- easy understandability and 'reason-ability' *

are interlinked (at least to a degree). If a program has bugs (i.e. is not accurate) it defeats the purpose, so efficiency does not count. It will merely be doing the wrong things more efficiently (does it remind you of a politician!). If it is accurate and efficient but very badly organized, (especially when it grows in size), making any change is likely to introduce bug (i.e. compromise accuracy).

* the phrase 'reason-ability' is something that I

introduced here, to mean - the quality of a program which renders it easy to reason with.

The last attribute however is probably a bit more subtle. *Why do we need to reason with a program easily?* Well, there are benefits, such as – if you can understand the pieces of the code, and how the fit together, like the back of your hand, you can easily unearth any obvious flaw, or any obvious scope of efficiency improvement. It's like looking at a somewhat organized drawing room and thinking – if only the sofa would move a wee bit to the right, it would look perfect. to make it more efficient. (And those are by far not the only benefits). We will embark upon the discussion in detail soon, albeit in a roundabout way. (Sometimes avoiding shortcuts make the journey more enjoyable.)

Putting two and two together

Object Oriented Programming came into prominence when procedural programming was already in place. One could imagine that there were problems that procedural programming style fell short to address.

There are plenty of discussion, I would think, for the reasons why Object Oriented Programming has an edge over procedural. Hiding unauthorized modification of data, abstraction, modularity, better organization and control, even easier modelling from real world. For instance, if you are developing a bus ticket reservation system, you can think of *Bus* as an entity with a number of seats, *Trips* as an entity associated with a *Bus. Passenger* as an entity with a name and contact number. *Ticket* as an entity with trip number, sit number, passenger name and price, and so on. It is perhaps comforting to think, that by emulating the objects (some aspect of them) in real world, your design task has become way easier.

For a moment consider that *computers are for computation*. One of the simplest computations I know is putting two and two together. If you are to write a program, which will do just that, how would you model it using objects from real world?

Would you create a *Bus* class and put a method *addTwoAndTwo* in there? Would you create a *Student* class? Does any real world object logically relate to a pure computation?

...

In my view – the short and simple answer is 'No'. When you are modelling something through an object, you may think about what operations you can do on that object (e.g. get the temperature of a cooking pot. *pot.getTemparature()*). Without the object - the operation in that case, is meaningless. However there are certain computational concepts, which can exist without real world objects backing them up (because computation has it's own domain, which is different from physical domain).

You can say 2 breads, or 2 glasses. But just the number 2 is a quantitative denomination, which may exist (conceptually) without being attached to glasses or breads. And 2 + 2 = 4, will equally apply to aggregating the count of glasses, and the count of breads.

...

The above discussion would suggest, that Object Oriented Modelling of computational behaviour, while very useful in some situations, is not a panacea for any type of computational modelling. Procedural programming, left to itself, on the other hand is monolithic. A computation may not always follow a rectilinear path (in a manner of speaking). And when a program involves more complicated web of execution pathways, procedural programming, unless specifically fitted for the purpose, is likely to become very difficult to reason with.

One way to simplify a possible design structure is to break it down into simpler parts. For a good design, broken down in such a manner, the parts should be structurally and functionally coherent as a unit, and it should be easily integrable with the main design. (Think of a well designed car. The gears and the engine, each has it's own function, and it's own place in the whole assembly).

Just because something is less than the whole (and at one point was included in the whole) it should not be considered a part. Think of a working gear taken out of a car during maintenance, and a piece of gear broken into multiple pieces. There is a not so fine line, between a part and a junk. Hence the point of (structural and functional) coherence. [No reasonable programmer would possibly, break a program, into modules, just based on their line numbers for instance. e.g. break a 100 line code into 20 modules, of 5 lines each, purely based on line numbers)].

...

While building a physical object, we can have units which we assemble. Think of a house, where a brick may be an unit, and so is the wash basin, which will be fitted in the bathroom. Naturally, while modelling a computation, it would be nice if we had computational units.

What would a computational unit do? It would possibly perform a part of the computation, based on some input, and finally producing some output. (And it should of course be pluggable to the whole). You might have already guessed, that I am driving at a function. (As an aside, could you think up of any other thing, which can be considered an unit of computation? - This question is not important for the discussion of this book, though).

So if we had the right tools to break a computation down

into convenient computational units (functions) and easily assemble those units into a whole (program) that would give us a means to model a pure computation properly. (at least a better means than Object Oriented Modelling would possibly offer). Functional Programming goes a long way to provide this set of tools.

Setting up the shop

Download

Scala is the choice of language in this book. As of today (17/10/2016) the official stable version seems to be 2.11.8 (It will require Java 1.6 or higher, already installed properly on the machine).

If you go to the page http://www.scala-lang.org/download/ in a browser, based on your operating system, (I have checked in Mac and an Windows VM), it shows up the correct download version link through a prominent button (towards the top of the page). For Windows it is .msi, and for Mac it is .tgz

You may also follow links on the page and choose your own version etc. for download.

For Windows

After downloading the msi, the same can be double-clicked, and then follow the prompts sensibly. (That should be good enough for installation). After installation is finished, if you open a command prompt and run the command

scala -version

you should see a message like below -

Scala code runner version 2.11.8 -- Copyright 2002-2016, LAMP/EPFL

For Mac

You can unzip the .tgz file, then copy the unzipped folder to some location of your choice (e.g. /<your home directory>/tools). For command line usage, put the bin directory of scala-2.11.8 in the path (in your .profile [or .bash_profile as the case may be] file). e.g.

export PATH=$PATH:~/tools/scala-2.11.8/bin

Then open a new terminal window and issue the command

scala -version

If you have right version of JDK (1.6 or above) and Scala properly installed, and path properly set, you should see a response like below -

Scala code runner version 2.11.8 -- Copyright 2002-2016, LAMP/EPFL

If you prefer to work with a different version : slight variation in Scala version should not matter for the exercises presented (and even the material presented) in this book. [Although, please note that the code in this book is largely tested on Scala 2.11.8]

And saying Hello

Although this book is not about teaching Scala language, from time to time some feature of the language may be discussed. (Usually) partly for the relevance of that feature in the discussion, and partly because, a bit of start on the language may help reading the book without frequently resorting to a Scala programming textbook or the internet for syntax or feature information.

...

For a 'Hello World' program in Scala - in your command

prompt go to the directory where you want to work in. In your file manager, create a file *abc.scala* in that directory, with the following content.

println("Hello World")

and save it. Issue the command -

scala abc.scala

in the command prompt, and you should see "Hello World" (without the quotes) printed in the console.

=>scala abc.scala

Hello World

REPL

In Scala, a development environment named REPL (full name - Read Eval Print Loop) is available. It is an interactive language shell - a sort of interpreter shell, for interactive evaluation of code.

If you just type scala in the command prompt and press enter, you should get it. (and to quit use Ctrl-D).

When you get into the shell the prompt changes to

scala>

As you type code lines in the shell and press enter, it executes the code (as it can) and also provides information about types etc.

It may go somewhat like this -

=>scala

Welcome to Scala 2.11.8 (Java HotSpot(TM) 64-Bit Server VM, Java 1.8.0_73).

Type in expressions for evaluation. Or try :help.

scala> println("abc")
abc

scala> val x = 2 + 2
x: Int = 4

scala>

This too will be useful in our journey.

Functional functions

Any programming, that is not functional programming, is not necessarily non-functional.

Functional Programming provide a set of tools to be able to organize a program in a certain fashion. What some of those tools are, will hopefully be clear as the book unfolds. But to start from a lower key (in a manner of speaking) i.e. to start from a somewhat clean slate of a mind, without burdened by too many pre-conceived ideas, (which may help discussing questions, which some may consider too simplistic) - consider for a moment, that we already have functions in both procedural and object oriented programming. Can we not use the same or similar functions, to organize our programs?

Well if we could, then it would not probably be named as Functional Programming. Then the next question is likely to be, why do we need different type of functions? This again is a question, which probably makes a very good case for a detailed answer (to the extent, that this also is another candidate for being expressed throughout much of the book).

It would be easier to tackle the question in a different way. Pick out on some of the ways the two types of functions differ (the one coming from say traditional Object Oriented Programming, and the ones applicable to Functional Programming which I am calling 'Functional Functions' [But in most part of the book, a function would simply refer to a 'Functional Function']), point by point, and what are the benefit(s) that can be materialized, because of that difference (improvement) in function type or function behaviour.

Higher Order Functions

The first point that can be mentioned (and the order has been picked rather arbitrarily), is that in Functional programming, functions can be higher order functions. This feature [if you prefer to call it that] is also known as First Class Functions, but somehow I like the term Higher Order Functions better. this essentially means, that the language, that supports functional programming, should support - passing functions as arguments to other functions, returning them as the values from other functions, and assigning them to variables or storing them in data structures.

This is already a handful (in a manner of speaking), and this is just the first point. Time to tackle it by the 'divide and rule' philosophy (which may be considered a nasty tool at the hands of some of the political parties, but nevertheless, is very useful in technical analysis).

Let's pick on the 'assigning them to variables' part.

Functions as variables

Functions can be treated very much like variables in Functional Programming. This has implication not just in assigning them to variables, and moving them around as a variable, but in other ways too. (For instance if it is a variable, it should have a type. But we will come to this later).

Let's pick on a simple function 'add' as defined below.

In a file (say 'f1.scala') write the following code and save it.

```scala
def add(a:Int, b: Int) : Int = {
    a + b;
}
```

println(add(2,2))

If you execute it, it will print 4 on the console.

There is not much to the function. The definition starts with def, the parameters with types, and the return type has been specified. Then the code starts after an equal sign. The actual code (within flower braces) has only one line. No statement like 'return' is specified. The result of execution of the last statement in a function, is by default the return value from the function.

Now consider the following code, which also prints 4 when run.

def add(a:Int, b: Int) : Int = {
a + b;
}

val x: (Int, Int) => Int = add

println(x(2,2))

What has happened is, we have assigned the function add to a variable named x, and then called the variable x (as if it was a function [which it was]) with the original arguments. It produced the same result.

The change may not look like much in terms of code volume, but the change has huge implications.

In order to explain the assignment (to the variable x), an introduction to function types may be in order.

Function types

If functions are to be treated as variables, it is natural that they should have types (as variables do [at least in some languages]). What should be the type of a function? How should it look like?

Remember that we mention the type of a variable, usually when it is defined (at least in Java and Scala). i.e. type is made explicit at variable definition. Extrapolating on the same concept, we can think that a function definition should include it's type. (And this is not far off).

A function definition shown in the code above (leaving aside the keyword def), may look like -

add(a:Int, b: Int) : Int

Leaving aside the names, and concentrating purely on types, we can say that this function takes two Int as arguments and returns an Int as a result. That is precisely it's type. Except that it's written as follows (syntactically) -

(Int, Int) => Int

The arrow kind of sign '=>' here, is perhaps to emphasise, that something results in something.

Note that while considering a function type, the internal operation of the function is immaterial (that is more a part of the function value, like a String type variable can hold any particular String as value). It is just what type(s) of variables it takes (and in what order), and what type of variable it returns. A subtract function, which similarly takes two integers, and returns the result of their subtraction, would be of the same type as this one.

Eventually, as we define a variable (an immutable one) holding an Int as -

val a: Int

we can define a function (of type *(Int, Int) => Int*) as -

val x: (Int, Int) => Int

and as we can assign a value to the Int variable as -

val a: Int = 2

we can assign a function value to the 'function variable' x as -

val x: (Int, Int) => Int = add

Note that add is a particular function (which is a function value) of the type (Int, Int) => Int , and hence can be assigned to a variable of that type. [it is like a particular String e.g "Hello" is a value (of type String), and hence, can be assigned to a variable of type String.]

Function as parameters to functions

A language supporting Higher Order Functions (Scala included), would also support functions being passed as parameters to another function. If you can come to think of functions as variables having types, this will not possibly be too far away.

It is probably easier to explain with an example.

```
def sum(a:Int, b:Int) : Int = {a + b}
def product(a:Int, b:Int) : Int = {a * b}
def printit(name:String, a:Int, b:Int, c:(Int, Int) => Int) : Unit = {
        println("The " + name + " of " + a + " and " + b + " is " +
c(a,b))
}
```

```
printit("sum",1,2,sum)
printit("product",3,2,product)
```

The above code, when run, produces -

The sum of 1 and 2 is 3
The product of 3 and 2 is 6

As you can see, the *printit* function takes a function of type *Int2Int* (which is an alias for any function that takes two Int and returns an Int) as it's fourth argument. Both sum and product are defined as functions of that type. Hence we can pass either of them and get a well formatted result.

How would you accomplish the same formatting without higher order functions? You will possibly have to write a case statement, or if else statement with two separate *println* statements. Or you might chose to write two functions one for each type of formatting.

If you wanted to augment the capability of the whole program by introducing a *div* function (division of one integer by another), in the old scheme (i.e. if you were using case for instance), it won't be easy to extend. But with the current structure, all you need to do is add the new function, and add a call to *printit*, with that function and other parameters, as required.

Pretty much, the addition of following two lines, to the above code will do -
def div(a:Int, b:Int) : Int = {a / b}
printit("div",4,2,div)

Easy extension of capability, don't you think!

Anonymous Functions
In a normal function (e.g. in a function in Java), you can pass a variable of a certain type (e.g. int), but you can also directly pass a value of that type.

Like you can call a function add (which takes two int arguments) as add(a,b) or as add(2,3).

When you pass functions as arguments, it should be possible to do something equivalent. Which is - to be able to pass a function value [which consists of the function parameters, the => sign, and the function code including the flower brackets enclosing the code (when required)], instead of the function name. i.e.

printit("sum",1,2, (a:Int, b:Int) => { a+b })

> instead of

printit("sum",1,2,sum)

> Which means your code may look like -

def printit(name:String, a:Int, b:Int, c:(Int, Int) => Int) : Unit = {
> *println("The " + name + " of " + a + " and " + b + " is " +*
c(a,b))
}

printit("sum",1,2, (a:Int, b:Int) => { a+b })
*printit("product",3,2, (a:Int, b:Int) => { a*b })*

> and behave (as you might have guessed) in the same way, as when you defined the function add, and product separately and called the *printit* function with their names.

The sum of 1 and 2 is 3
The product of 3 and 2 is 6

> This is how anonymous functions work.

> If you are using the function, such as add, only in one place, it may save the hassle of formally defining the function. But this is not necessarily the only use case for it. Anonymous Functions (the feature) is a powerful tool at your disposal, and within the permitted syntax and semantics of it, you may choose to use it any the which way you like.

> By the way, in Scala, the semicolon is optional unless you are righting contiguous statements in the same block within the same line. i.e. something like

> { a+b; c *d}. Also flower braces are optional when only one statement is involved in the block. Hence the following is good enough (no flower braces around a+b) -

printit("sum",1,2, (a:Int, b:Int) => a+b)

and so is the following -

def sum(a:Int, b:Int) : Int = a + b

Even the following works for the definition of *printit* given earlier -

printit("sum",1,2,(a, b) => a+b)

Here the type of *a* and *b* as input parameters, is omitted [(a,b) instead of (a:Int, b:Int)]. This is possible as *a* and *b* is already bound to Int type from the definition of *printit* function (as it's second and third argument – see explanation below).

Explanation : The function signature of printit is -

def printit(name:String, a:Int, b:Int, c:(Int, Int) => Int) : Unit

So the 2nd and 3rd arguments are Int. If the fourth argument, which is a function [which takes two int arguments], gets passed a, and b directly within the function body of printit function, i.e. something like -

println("The " + name + " of " + a + " and " + b + " is " + c(a,b))

then there is no doubt that the function c has got the right type of input arguments (because a, and b are Int – by definition [because they are 2nd and 3rd arguments of the printit function]).

If, instead of a named function like c, an anonymous function is used (of type which takes two Int arguments as input), and still a, and b are passed as arguments to that anonymous function, the inference does not change.

Scala can infer a lot of things (types included) from the context.

Functions within functions

Like it is possible to define a local variable within a

normal function, it is possible to define a local function within a higher order function.

Consider the following code -

```
def factorial(n:Int) : Int = {
        def go(x:Int) : Int = {
                if (x <= 0) 1
                else x * go (x-1)
        }

        go(n)
}

println(factorial(5))
```

Here the function *go* is local to the factorial function. It is being called with the value originally passed to the *factorial* function, and calculates the factorial recursively.

...

Incidentally, since the function *go*, consists of a single statement, it could have been written without the flower braces.

```
def factorial(n:Int) : Int = {
        def go(x:Int) : Int = if (x <= 0) 1 else x * go (x-1)

        go(n)
}

println(factorial(5))
```

The function factorial could have been written, without the inner function. However the above, serves as an illustration of local functions (function definition within function definition).

As a direct recursive function, definition of factorial could be written as -

*def factorial(n:Int) : Int = if (n <= 0) 1 else n * factorial (n-1)*

Functions as return values

A higher order function can return another function, as a return value. In the following code -

```
def doubleIt(x:Int) : Int = x * 2
def tripleIt(x:Int) : Int = x * 3
def same(x:Int) : Int = x

def foo(n:Int) : Int => Int = {
        if (n == 2) doubleIt
        else if (n == 3) tripleIt
        else same
}

val bar : Int => Int = foo(3)
println(bar(4))
```

which prints 12 on the console when run, the return type of the function foo is a function (of type *Int => Int,* meaning any function that takes a single Int as argument and returns an Int). Clearly the functions *doubleIt, tripleIt* and *same,* all are functions of that type.

Foo takes an Int, and depending on the value of that, it decides which of those three functions it should return as it's return value. A call to foo(3) will return the function tripleIt (which in this case is assigned to *bar*). *bar* then is essentially a copy of tripleIt. And hence a call to *bar(4)* will triple it's argument and return 12.

Note that we could have written it with anonymous functions as -

```
def foo(n:Int) : Int => Int = {
        if (n == 2) (x) => x * 2
```

```
        else if (n == 3) x => x * 3
        else x => x
}
```

```
val bar : Int => Int = foo(3)
println(bar(4))
```

Note that since x is the only parameter in those anonymous functions defined within foo, we can get away with not putting braces around x (input parameter) [such as in the *n == 3* case in the above code].

Note also that in the above definition of the function *foo*, what is actually retuned is not an Int value but an anonymous function [either of - *(x) => x * 2, x => x * 3 or x => x* based on the value of n]. And only when an Int value (e.g. 4) is applied to that (returned) function, it returns an Int value (upon evaluating the function).

Storing functions in data structures

In HOF (higher order function) context, it is also possible to store functions in data structures, like having an Array of functions (as you can have Array of Int) each element of which will be a function of certain type.

But before that, a little discussion about how Scala Arrays work.

You can define an initialise an Array of Ints simply as -

val x = Array(3,5,7)

And then access the first element of the array (Scala arrays use zero-based index, so 1st element is with index 0, second element is with index 1 and so on), simply as x(0).

A quick verification in REPL would run like this -

```
scala> val x = Array(3,5,7)
x: Array[Int] = Array(3, 5, 7)

scala> println(x(0))
3

scala> x(0)
res1: Int = 3

scala>
```

Good thing about REPL is it shows types of variables (as shown above).

Note that the type of the Array is Array[Int] (i.e. an Array of Int elements), which has been inferred, since the elements assigned to the Array was of type Int.

It is possible to explicitly define the type of the elements while declaring the Array value. e.g.

val x: Array[Int] = Array(1,2,3)

Eventually if you initialised an array (whose type has not been specified) with Strings, it would be an Array of Strings.

```
scala> val y = Array("one","two","three")
y: Array[String] = Array(one, two, three)
```

And if you wanted to see what happens if you define an array (not explicitly typed) with one Int and one String value, -

```
scala> val z = Array(1,"one")
z: Array[Any] = Array(1, one)
```

It resolves to an Array of type Any .(It has to do with the type hierarchy of Scala. It tries to find a common ground, so to speak).

...

Note it is also possible to initialise an empty array with –

Array().
scala> val x = Array()
x: Array[Nothing] = Array()

scala> val x : Array[Int] = Array()
x: Array[Int] = Array()

As you might note, if the Array type is not explicitly defined, in this case, it resolves to an Array of Nothing.

If the type is explicitly declared however, there is no such issue.

...

An Array of functions, can be defined with the function type as array elements type, e.g.

val f : Array[(Int, Int) => Int] = Array()

can define an Array of functions which, (each of which), takes two Ints and returns an Int.

In order to initialise the Array with some functions, you could either use predefined functions of that type, or you could use anonymous functions (and eventually a combination of both is also ok). See the run in REPL below.

scala> def sum(a:Int, b:Int) : Int = a +b
sum: (a: Int, b: Int)Int

scala> def subt(a:Int, b:Int) : Int = a -b
subt: (a: Int, b: Int)Int

scala> val f : Array[(Int, Int) => Int] = Array(sum,subt,(a:Int, b:Int) => a*b)
f: Array[(Int, Int) => Int] = Array(<function2>, <function2>, <function2>)

Eventually the individual functions can simply be

accessed with array indices (as if they were variables). For instance f(2) refers to the third function in the array (which is an anonymous function in this case, and is effectively product of the two integer arguments).

Hence calling the f(2) function, with two integer arguments will yield the product of those two integers (Int).

scala> f(2)(3,4)
res3: Int = 12

Here f(2) is the function being called with the set of arguments 3 and 4.

...

After the initial discussion on higher order functions, let us turn into another very important aspect of functional programming. (The second point, if you prefer).

Referential Transparency

Definition?
Referential Transparency is of course an attribute, that makes something referentially transparent. It is more convenient to define something as referentially transparent, than to define the attribute itself. [Just as (I guess), explaining sweetness to someone, gets easier, if you let him eat some sugar, and then say, 'something which tastes like sugar has sweetness'.]

...

In terms of the definition of Referentially Transparent, what I found akin to an official definition (or perhaps that *is* the official definition), is -

An expression is said to be referentially transparent if it can be replaced with its value without changing the behaviour of a program.

...

There are other definitions (slightly different versions), but in essence they do not refute the above definition. But I did not find any of them (that I have paid attention to), to be more suitable starting point for my explanation [especially from easy understandability point of view].

...

Before I elaborate further on the definition, In the following (two) subsections, I am attempting to give a perspective on the words, **referential** and **transparency**, which may help understand, why the attribute may be so named (and it may also help remembering it's meaning). In the third subsection, I will get down to explaining the definitions.

Referential

You may have an idea, that it talks about a reference (or something related to that). The dictionary definition is *'Containing or of the nature of references or allusions.'*

But what does referential mean in this context?

Think of a program p [as shown below. (very-) pseudo code], which calls a function f, multiple times, with different set of arguments.

begin

    assignment a
    expression b

    f(1, 2) # first call

    expression c

    f(3, 3) # second call

assignment d
expression e

f(5,1) # third call

return g
end

Suppose also the function is defined, somewhat like (again in pseudo code) -

def f (a, b) {
    if (a+b) == 0
        then a * b
    else
        a *b / (a+b)
}

The function call in some sense is a *reference* to the code in the function body. And hence the function body is the *referent*. And the thing that contains the reference in this case is the program. *So the program references the function code (code in the function body), through the function call.*

Note that, if we were to replace the function calls, with the actual code from the function body, the replacement will not be complete - unless we replace the arguments *a* and *b*, with their corresponding value for each call. E.g. For the first call to the function in the program, the replacement would be somewhat like -

{
    if (1+2) == 0
        then 1 * 2
    else
        1 *2 / (1+2)

}

because for the first call the argument values are 1 and 2. (And *a*, and *b*, being arguments to the function, has meaning only to the function. As far as the program is concerned, the variables could have been named *c* and *d*, instead of *a* and *b* [it absolutely does not matter to the program, so long as it can pass two Int values as arguments to the function, while calling it).

...

Once again : *The program references the function code, through the function call.*

Transparency
While using a language, sometimes people start moulding it in ways, which renders a meaning just opposite to what it was originally intended. Or opposite words take on similar meaning in some context.

One such example is, when many young people describe looks, metaphorically, in terms of state of coldness. Imagine a young person describing someone as "She is hot." or "He is cool". Whatever he may mean, it is quite likely that, in those two sentences, the words *hot* and *cool*, have very similar connotation. Although in terms of original dictionary meaning, they are words, which means rather opposite states of temperature.

Transparency is another such example.

In a general sense, Transparency is an attribute, that makes something, clear and lucent. A transparent object is something, that does not hide something behind it. So in that sense, when used metaphorically, it should mean something, that is not hiding anything, aka non-deceptive.

However in managerial jargon in business (especially in

IT project governance), it is used quiet often to mean - something that hides completely what is behind it.

For instance - something should be 'Transparent to the user' may mean that something should be presented to the user, in such a manner, that user need not know (and should not have a clue in any case), where the thing is sourced from.

Suppose a telephone company, or a bank, has call centres, in New York, Shanghai, Manilla, and Mumbai. And suppose the customers are given a single hotline number, to lodge their service difficulties. When the manager says 'where the call is being responded from, should be transparent to the customer', what he may roughly mean is -

– The caller should be talking to someone with a Christian first name, like Albert or Alicia (whatever their real name is)

– The caller should be greeted with very similar greeting such as 'Good day Sir,' [or Madam as the case may be], 'How was your day so far'.

– And the respondent should be speaking in perfect American accent.

That may not necessarily be the case in reality, however, my point is the phrase 'transparent to the customer', quite likely means this scenario, in the context.

…

For better or for worse, the word *transparency* in *referential transparency,* has taken on this opposite connotation. In context of functional programming, this word means, something, that hides completely. It roughly means (in this context), that -

– the program, which references the function body,

through the function call, should be oblivious, (should be completely in the dark , if you prefer), as to

    —   whether the function calls (any of the calls), is retained as they are (i.e. retained as function call), or

    —   whether the function call is *actually replaced* by the evaluated value (after evaluating with corresponding parameter values),

    —   and should still expect the outcome to be unaffected.

Explanation (of definition)

Let's start with the original definition.

An expression is said to be referentially transparent if it can be replaced with its value without changing the behaviour of a program.
...

Firstly - note that it talks about an expression (and not about a function as such). That makes it more broad than a function in some sense. Any expression, fulfilling appropriate conditions, could be referentially transparent. (A function could also be considered as an expression).

Consider the expression { x * (x +3) }. This is an expression, but this really expresses a function of x in a sense.

Secondly – it talks about a program. Presumably, a program where the expression is used (or the function is called). Although that fact could have been more explicit, in the definition.

Thirdly – it talks about replacing the function call with the corresponding value. This again could have been more explicit. Besides it should apply to all calls of the function, jointly and severally (as they mention in legal contracts) in the program, not just one.

i.e. If in a program, a function [say f(x) which is defined as *x * (x +3)] is called, (say) 3 times, in different locations, once with the argument 1, once with 2 and once with 5, and if you replace the first call with 4, and/or the second call with 10, and/or the third call with 40, the program should still evaluate to the same value or effect.*

Note that, for a program behaviour, the final result is definitely a part. But it may also include side effects, such as printing a message in the log. So consideration for alteration of meaning for a program, may include such side effects.

i.e. if because of a replacement of a function with it's value, the program somehow stopped printing informational messages to the log file (but giving the correct final output), the meaning of the program can be considered changed, and hence the referential transparency is broken.

However it really depends on the designated objective of the program, as to whether such alteration of side effects, will be considered meaningful or not. For instance, if the log messages are not considered of any importance for the overall functioning of the program, then in spite of such alterations, the RT may be considered unbroken in this case.

However if there is no alteration even in side effects, then it (the function) is definitely referentially transparent.

...

Why RT is necessary?

Let me explain why RT is made so much fuss about, in functional programming.

Suppose we have a function defined as -

def f (a, b) {
   if (a+b) == 0
          then a * b
   else

$$a * b / (a+b)$$

}

Consider the program p (which uses the function), is defined as (in pseudo-code) -

begin

$r = 5$

expression a

$f(1, -1)$ # first call

expression b

$f(3, 3)$ # second call

expression c

$r = r * f(-2, 2)$ # third call

return r

end

As the program stands now, if someone were to ask you to take a guess at, what would be the return value of the program – you would probably not take long to evaluate it.

What would be the opposite behaviour?

Suppose the function f is defined instead as (in pseudo-code) -

def f (a, b) {

if $(a+b) == 0$

then $a * b * r$

else

$a * b / (a+b)$

}

[consider that the function is defined within the program, and hence it has access to the program variable r]

Now it is no longer so easy to evaluate the whole program. And the main program code body (without the function definition) is 8 lines (10 if you consider begin and end). Think what would happen if it was 80 lines of code (let alone any bigger than that).

Hence, if we can somehow reason about the function value in isolation, it makes the job of evaluation (of the whole program) much easier. And if you consider, that the program itself may be like a function or an expression, in a greater context – then the same can be said about reasoning with the program's overall evaluation, against the backdrop of that greater context.

Which leads to the first (and perhaps foremost) benefit of having Referentially Transparent functions. Which is *'piece reliability'*, (or *'reliability of modularity of action'* if you prefer).

'piece reliability'
or *'reliability of modularity of action'*

A program (or a 'logical unit of code' if you prefer to call it that), is a composition of computation. Sometimes a composition of complex interweaving pieces of computations. A functional decomposition, among other things, is meant to decompose the complex, interweaving computational composition, into smaller pieces of computation, and to restructure the bigger computation, as an assembly of the smaller pieces. This provides better structure, and with it comes better understandability and robustness. A well structured and organised code is easier to understand and debug, than a cluttered one. [And eventually – avoidance of code duplication, and corresponding code compactness also comes with it].

...

In this sense – a function may be considered as *a designated piece of action* or *a designated piece of computation* (or *a designated module of computation* if you prefer), and RT essentially states that – *whether you refer to a function (which is a designated piece of computation) by it's call, or by it's evaluated value, the result should be the same, irrespective of it's context of call in the program.*

...

The overall program then is a (computational) composition of smaller pieces of computation. To reason about the functional integrity of the overall (composed) structure, (which is the program), and to guarantee the reliability of the outcome - the individual pieces must be reliable. (They should not change their colour with season – in a manner of speaking. When you put the gear handle of your car, in neutral position, you expect the car to be on neutral, without fail, otherwise the result could be disastrous).

Think of building a toy crane with Lego pieces. You are building a (toy) crane by joining pre-fabricated pieces. If you have no doubt about the structural integrity of the pieces themselves, all you need to worry about, is where and how, you stick one piece, with another suitable piece, to get the overall structure in shape. Now imagine doing the same with computational pieces.

[Note : this 'piece reliability', is a necessary but not a sufficient condition for the overall structural integrity – the fault may lie in the way they have been assembled]

So the first, and possibly the greatest benefit, is reliability of computational assembly, and ease with which such a computational assembly could be reasoned about.

Note : This concept of referential transparency, and reasoning about overall program easily, by (conceptually) substituting function calls with corresponding values - is also known as the 'substitution model'. The key here is the ability to substitute, with guarantee of no repercussion in overall outcome.

...

memoization

Memoization is yet another benefit of having RT functions.

In computing, memoization is an optimization technique used primarily to speed up computer programs by storing the results of expensive function calls, and returning the cached result when the same inputs occur again.

In other words, suppose you have a polynomial function which takes an argument and returns the calculated result. Something like -

f(x) = 12.5 * power(x,4) + 10.3 * cube(x) + 8.2 * sqr(x) + 2 * x + 9.3

If you have total 20 calls to the function from the program, and each one is either with the argument 2.6 or 13, you can evaluate the function values with those two arguments at one place, and safely replace the calls with one of the corresponding values (based on the argument for the call). You would save considerable computation time and resource, in terms of percentage. [For a small code it may not be apparent, but for a very large program execution (or execution with a large amount of data) it is likely to be a good difference].

order of execution

If your functions are referentially transparent, you do not need to worry about their order of execution, so long as their value is available at the point where they are needed. This is a great advantage for parallelisation of computing.

You could evaluate them in a completely different thread (or threads) and collect the value, before the main program execution proceeds from that point. You may even be able to parallelise the main code execution on a different thread [at least partially – e.g. up to the first call to the function in the program, and then wait on the completion of evaluation of function, with that call's arguments].

lazy evaluation

It is possible for the overall program, based on it's arguments etc. - to go through such an execution path, that it won't call the function with some arguments. (e.g. [in context of the above example, of polynomial function] say only 2 of the 20 calls to the function is to be executed, and both of those calls have argument 2.6]). In such cases, with good planning of execution, you can get away with not evaluating the function for the argument 13 at all. That is also saving on computational resource.

Lazy evaluation refers to evaluation of a function or expression only at the point of it's first invocation. Hence, if it is not invoked even once, in the context of the overall program execution, it will not be evaluated at all.

and what is program

Note - each program itself (even the overall program), in a bigger scheme of things, could be considered as a function or expression (in other words 'a module of execution', for another, larger context of computation). In that sense it would be a good idea to build it (the overall program itself), as mush as possible, following functional programming conventions - such that, at a later time, if this is required to act as part of a larger whole, this piece could have the reliability, that is expected of an individual function (to the extent possible).

In the wilderness

Although referential transparency is defined, in the context of the whole program, it is not trivial to determine whether the function is referentially transparent, by looking at the program. When you are looking at the whole program – you are in a sense already in the wilderness, (and if the function is not referentially transparent, you lost the piece reliability already).

Looking at it another way, in order to determine whether a ball bearing in a car, is of the right size and specification, you should examine the ball bearing and not the car. You may argue, that if it fits in place and the car runs right, then it must be of the right size. It may be so. But imagine, if you needed to drive the car, whose brake system may or may not be fitted correctly. If the execution follows happy path (i.e. fitting to specification) everything works well, but if that is not the case ...

Making sure the ball bearing is right, by examining the ball bearing (and not the car), translates in our case, to making sure that the function is referentially transparent, by looking at the the function itself (and not the program). A function is guaranteed to be referentially transparent if it is a *pure function*. [In this sense purity of a function has somewhat causal (cause to consequence) relation with referential transparency of that function. Purity of a function is the cause that as a consequence, guarantees it's referential transparency]. And because judging the purity of a function is easier, and more direct way of reaching referential transparency - in a sense following purity of function is more important than trying to follow referential transparency.

Referential Transparency is the guarantee (in a sense, the name of the contract), that enables substitution model. And purity of function guarantees referential transparency. So focussing on purity of function is more inside out (and more definitive) approach, towards building functionally coherent computational assembly.

Pure functions

In computer programming, a function may be considered a pure function if both of the following statements about the function hold:

The function result value cannot depend on any hidden information or state that may change while program execution proceeds or between different executions of the program, nor can it depend on any external input from I/O devices.

Evaluation of the result does not cause any semantically observable side effect or output, such as mutation of mutable objects or output to I/O devices.

Looking at it another way, *a pure function has it's input parameters as it's sole variants, and it's return value as it's sole effect.*

...

To explain it further, consider that a function (at least in mathematical sense) is essentially a mapping from the input domain to the output domain.

e.g. a function f(x: Int) = x * x, maps from a domain of integers, to points in a domain of square of integers. Intuitively, if it is pure function, it would do just that. [i.e. just connect a point from the input domain, to the corresponding point in the output domain], without asking for anything more than the input it is designed to expect, and causing no other observable effect to the external world than the output it is designed to produce.

Note that as part of the processing, it may use constants (such as PI), or may call other functions in turn. [For ease of discussion, let us consider for the moment that those functions would be pure too]. However it can not use any other variant (such as a state which may change from call to call, or run to run). And it can not have any other observable external effect, such as mutating the state of mutable variable, (or printing something out to the console).

[*In this respect, note that – the program designer may decide, that based on the context, a certain type of output – say writing to a log file, is irrelevant while considering the purity of function for that context. In this case, for that context, a function may be considered pure even when it produces such output. In an absolute theoretical context, such a function may not meet the criteria of a pure function. However in practical programmatic context this could still be considered a pure function. The key in this case, of course is conscious choice.*

Making such a decision, of course, should be accompanied by careful thought, that the allowance inadvertently did not cause the alteration of intended behaviour, of the overall outcome]

...

A pure function is complete guarantee of (it's) Referential Transparency. And as I already mentioned, it is easier to check purity of function, than to directly track it's referential transparency.

Immutability

Immutability of parameters (and by extension output – [because, one functions output may very well be passed to another function as input]), is very important for pure functions. If certain objects or collection of objects are to be shared through a chain of functions - at any given point in the processing chain, a function working with it, should have the guarantee that it has not been unpredictably tampered with, at any other point in the call chain. This has bearing on purity of the overall function call chain.

Think of a scenario e(f(g(h(x))). the variable x is going

through a sequence of processing, if somehow, the function h makes a change to x, that g has no way of knowing, then the result the function g hands over, may be unpredictable (at least from g's point of view) [*Note that the function g may be designed and written by someone other than the author of function h – and they may have no direct communication. In a functional programming development scenario, only things a developer should pretty much need to know is – the input and output types, and what processing needs to be done to the inputs to get to the output. He need not (and ideally should not have to) consider any history of the input variables, beyond what is passed on to him (i.e. to the function)*].

This problem could be completely avoided (the problem is denied at it's source, so to speak), if all the parameters and return values were to be immutable.

Scala promotes *val* (values -immutable), as opposed to *var* variables, by default. Collection also usually are immutable and has mutable counterparts for when they may be needed.

If you were to add 3 to the input (an Int) of a function [e.g. f(a) = a + 3], the return is another Int (a new value) created by adding 3 to the input Int. If it is a collection (say a List), and you are to take out the head (first element), and return the tail (the rest of elements) – the tail would be a new list (a new value) consisting of elements from 2nd one (of original List) onwards.

Unless specifically required, values need not be copied around, and once a value is used up, corresponding variable (where the value was held) can be ready for garbage collection.

Types, functions, and classes – a little more Scala

"Never forget 3 types of people in your life -
1.   *Those who helped you in your difficult times*
2.   *Those who left you in your difficult times*
3.   *Those who put you in your difficult times"*

In this chapter I would like to explain, usually through examples, a few finer points (conventions, syntactic conveniences, ...) - that Scala offers, and we may put to good use in Functional Programming. They may not readily relate to core functional concepts, but they are tools [certain types of kicks, punches and blocks – to draw on martial arts analogy], that can be used effectively, to your convenience, in both functional and non-functional coding. [*The basic focus is not on non-functional, but if something is learnt on the way to FP, which helps non-functional programming also, no harm in that*]

...

Types are important. *Type safety* is important. In real life (philosophically speaking), if you can ascertain the type of a person you will have to deal with, it becomes so much easier. On the other hand having completely misplaced trust on someone could end in a disaster.

In programming too, it is much easier and safer (especially safer), to deal with variables, whose type you know on the outset, and whose type can not change unpredictably.

Scala is a statically typed and type inferred language. In Scala, a value (val) or variable (var) can have only one type [and I am not talking here about clever rigging of the type in mysterious ways], and this is checked at compile time, and fixed through the lifetime of the variable or value. As far as possible, Scala infers the type of variables, from the usage context [e.g.

when you assign 3 to a *val*, it would infer the type of the *val* as Int], so you won't have to always declare the type explicitly in many cases. This saves a lot of typing [i.e. typing on keyboard]

The importance of typing

Possibly the biggest advantage of typing variables (and values), is type safety. Once you know the type of something, you would know (to some extent), how to deal with it, and what to expect from it. You would know when you add two Strings, you merely concatenate them, whereas, when you add two Ints, you are actually adding two numeric values in an arithmetical way.

Enforcing type safety static way, a lot of errors, and potential discrepancy can be caught during compile time. (Saving a lot of headache - in a manner of speaking).

In a more subtle way, setting type of a variable, or a function, at the outset, makes explicit, your intention of the expected behavioural standard from that variable or function. And that is a great deal in program design, and later understanding of program intention.

For instance – when I define a function, which takes in 2 Ints and returns an Int, you might guess that the function does some arithmetic calculation with those values and returns the result. Whereas if I were to define a function, which takes an Int and provides a String, you would probably guess that it is unlikely to be performing an arithmetic operation. (It would more likely be concatenating the Int and String value to create a formatted String, for instance.)

The more specific you can make the type of something, (in a way) the more information you have about it. And that makes it's behaviour that much more predictable, and dealing with it (in some sense) that much easier.

...

As this is not a textbook of Scala language itself, I am not going to discuss major individual types of Scala (such as Int, Double, String) in detail. But the mode of discussion (with Functional Programming being the goal of use in the backdrop) - will be more towards some special types, some nuances of the type system itself, and their usage in broader terms.

Scala types in general

Non-primitive types

This is possibly relevant to mention here, that unlike Java, Scala do not have any primitive types. Even an *Int* in Scala is a full fledged type with it's own API (Note the capital 'I' in *Int*. It is the same with *Boolean* and *Char* also).

And hence, you can call methods on an Int value (such as 3) with a . sign, such as

scala> val x = 3.equals(4)
x: Boolean = false

and can get away with it.

Type inference

I have already mentioned this briefly. Let's see some examples.

If you don't provide type to a value, and it is inferable (not going into the detail of this right now, but let's say for now – if it's readily inferable [possibly this is something that would unfold in the course of the book]), Scala infers it.

scala> val y = 2

y: Int = 2

You can also provide it explicitly.

scala> val z:Int = 3

z: Int = 3

But if it is explicitly specified and the value does not

match the type, then it will complaint.

scala> val n:String = 4

<console>:11: error: type mismatch;

 found   : Int(4)

 required: String

    val n:String = 4

        ^

Not a pretty site.

Immutability of value

If you declare something as *var* (variable), you can assign new values (of the same type) to it.

scala> *var a = 2*

a: Int = 2

scala> *a = 3*

a: Int = 3

However for a *val* (value) that is not acceptable.

scala> *val b = 4*

b: Int = 4

scala> *b = 5*

<console>:12: error: reassignment to val

    b = 5

    ^

Nor is it ok to assign value of a different type to a var.

scala> a = "xyz"

<console>:12: error: type mismatch;

found   : String("xyz")

required: Int

*   a = "xyz"*

*   ^*

Type aliasing

You can define alias for a type. The syntax is

type <alias-name> = actual type
e.g.
scala> type Integer = Int
defined type alias Integer

scala> val ab: Integer = 4
ab: Integer = 4

(Although Integer being a class in Java, and noting that Scala runs on JVM, such an alias name is far from a wise choice. But you get the idea).

...

Type aliasing is not just limited to variables. You can do the same with function types too.

For instance -
scala> type intpairtoint = (Int,Int) => Int
defined type alias intpairtoint

scala> def sum(a: Int, b:Int): Int = a + b
sum: (a: Int, b: Int)Int

scala> val f1: intpairtoint = sum
f1: intpairtoint = <function2>

In this case, the alias *intpairtoint* indicates a type of functions which take two Int as arguments and outputs a single Int. 'sum' as defined above, is such a function, and hence can be assigned to a value of type *intpairtoint*.

...

(a note on)

Placeholder syntax

Scala offers a syntax whereby underscores can be used as placeholders for one or more parameters, so long as each of them (the parameters represented by underscores in the function body) are used only once in the function body. This makes a lot of heavily used functions in FP (such as reduce) quite short and elegant. It also has use in the context of partially applied functions.

These parameters, indicated by the placeholders, are applied in the function body in the order in which they appear in the parameter list. The type of the variable also have to be unambiguously determined from the context, otherwise the type have to be mentioned.

...

Here is another example of defining a function of type *intpairtoint*, using the alias and *placeholder syntax*.

*scala> val product: intpairtoint = _ * _*
product: intpairtoint = <function2>

scala> product(2,3)
reso: Int = 6

Note that in this case, it is unambiguous that both the parameters are Int. (Elsewhere, in a different context, while discussing partially applied functions, type of such a parameter is explicitly defined).

...

Imagine how helpful such convention of syntax could be.

If you had a lot of different functions, each of which takes say 10 arguments of different types (but in particular order) and provides output of a particular type, defining an alias on it would save a lot of typing.

(Note that, although quite often, short code and clarity goes hand in hand – especially when the short code abstracts the essence of the processing, leaving behind the verbosity – if the programming clarity demands you to be explicit about something [and thus ditch the alias, for the more explicit declaration for instance], it is advisable that you give priority to clarity over brevity).

...

Needless to say, this applies to classes too.

```
scala> class Person(firstName: String, lastName:String, address:
String)
defined class Person

scala> type Student = Person
defined type alias Student

scala> val firstBoy: Student = new Student("John", "Dolka", "15
Andheri Road")
firstBoy: Student = Person@1fb700ee
```

Polymorphic functions

Usually for a function - the types of parameters (in the right order) and the return type, taken together - forms the type of the function. For instance a function 'isEqual' may be of type : (Int, Int) => Boolean . However at times, you may want, some or all of the types (of parameters and return value) for a function to be parametrizable, (i.e. type itself to be parametrizable)

For instance you may want to define 'isEqual' the same way for two Int, two Float, two Double and two Long values. i.e.

57

isEqual for Int would take two Int as argument and return a Boolean (based on whether the argument values are equal or not), isEqual for Floats would take two Float as arguments and return a Boolean, and so on. So long as the processing is defined the same way, except for the types, it would be nice to have the function defined once, but be able to parametrize on the type (of either argument). This is what a polymorphic function does.

Note: 1. It corresponds, in some sense, to the generic methods in Java.

    2. It has no relation with polymorphism as applied to Object Oriented Design

So instead of defining -

scala> def isEqual(a:Int, b:Int) = a == b

isEqual: (a: Int, b: Int)Boolean

  and

scala> def isEqual(a:Float, b:Float) = a == b

isEqual: (a: Float, b: Float)Boolean

  You could just define a single function as -

scala> def isEqual[T](a:T, b:T) = a == b

isEqual: [T](a: T, b: T)Boolean

  and this becomes a polymorphic function.

Type Constructors

  You might have come across different data structures such as Array, List or Set. Take an *Array* for instance. An Array is a collection, and it has to be an Array of something. (E.g Array of Int, Array of String etc.). So *Array* by itself is not a complete type. It takes another argument (type argument) to indicate the whole type of a variable. e.g. Array[Int], Array[String] etc. In this sense Array is a type constructor. It constructs a type by taking in a type, as argument. (and so are Set, List etc.)

Note that a type constructor can take more than one type argument. For example Map[String, Int]

Polymorphic functions and type constructors
It is possible to have type constructors with polymorphic functions, which abstracts over the underlying type of the constructor. For instance -

scala> def getElem[T](a: Array[T], i:Int) : T = a(i)

getElem: [T](a: Array[T], i: Int)T

The function 'getElem' is really redundant from efficacy point of view (you can just access an element of an array the usual way). However it demonstrates the way of polymorphic functions with type constructors. T could be any type, and the mechanism should work. Here are some examples -

scala> val x = Array(1,2,3)

x: Array[Int] = Array(1, 2, 3)

scala> val y = Array("a","b","c")

y: Array[String] = Array(a, b, c)

scala> val z = getElem(y,1)

z: String = b

scala> val u = getElem(x,2)

u: Int = 3

That was somewhat limited discussion about Types. Although there is far more to Scala types than this, and we would possibly revisit the subject with more advanced topics later on, but for now it is better to cover wider grounds, to build up the basis, on which deeper study of particular topics may be built upon.

Classes

Although classically classes are related to more object oriented side of a language, (and it is possible to write entire set of Scala codes, without explicitly defining a class within it) - to have some basic understanding of class syntax in Scala on the outset, makes a lot of things quicker, later on.

Since this is not a text book of Scala per se, the focus will be very basic syntax and interesting trick(s) [more as a refresher – so that you don't need to open another book or internet in a hurry] .

If you revisit the Java class, from the case study in the first chapter -

```
class Txn {


        private int acct;
        private Double amt;


        public Txn(String acctStr, String amtStr) {
                this.acct = Integer.parseInt(acctStr);
                this.amt = Double.parseDouble(amtStr);

        }
```

```
public int getAcct() {

    return acct;

}

public Double getAmt() {

    return amt;

}

}
```

It is a rather minimal class with constructor, and getters (and no setters). It could very easily be replaced with a one liner in Scala -

scala> class Txn(val acct:Int, val amt:Double)

defined class Txn

(Notice the keyword val in front of the parameter names).

And an instance of it, can be created as -

scala> val txn1 = new Txn(120, 23.65)

txn1: Txn = Txn@470e2030

And the members of that instance can be accessed as shown -

scala> println("balance of account " + txn1.acct + " is " + txn1.amt)

balance of account 120 is 23.65

A class can have var members too (but not encouraged).

scala> class Acct(val num:Int, var balance:Double)

defined class Acct

scala> val acct2 = new Acct(12, 25.50)

acct2: Acct = Acct@687080dc

scala> acct2.balance = 20.45

acct2.balance: Double = 20.45

scala> println("Ac " + acct2.num + " has a balance of " +
acct2.balance + " dollars.")

Ac 12 has a balance of 20.45 dollars.

Classes can take default value for (construction) parameters.

scala> class Acct(val num:Int, var balance:Double = 100.00)

defined class Acct

scala> val acct = new Acct(12)

acct: Acct = Acct@799d4f69

scala> println("Ac " + acct.num + " has a balance of " +
acct.balance + " dollars.")

Ac 12 has a balance of 100.0 dollars.

It can come very handy while extending classes, when all the subclasses will need to have one member of the superclass fixed.

scala> class Person(

| val id: Int,

| val name: String,

| val profession: String)

defined class Person

scala> class Teacher(

   | id: Int,

   | name:String,

   | subject:String) extends Person(id: Int, name: String, "teaching")

defined class Teacher

scala> val mathTeacher = new Teacher(1, "James Turner", "Math")

mathTeacher: Teacher = Teacher@18209303

scala> println("Occupation of " + mathTeacher.name + " is " + mathTeacher.profession)

Occupation of James Turner is teaching

Tuples

In all of the above examples, there is no internal method in the classes. They are used purely as assorted data structures – (like each row of a table). In traditional object oriented paradigm, even for such a structure you would need a class (and methods such as getters and setters – unless the language offer better shortcuts or alternatives).

Quiet often, in such assorted structures of data (data rows), we may not have a specific need to name the variables (columns) at each position. For instance we may not care whether the first field in the class Person (as shown above) is named *id*, or *serial* or anything else. We just need that to be an

Int. In such cases, you may fall back on tuples in Scala.

On a good day (actually any day) you need not even define the individual types of the members. You just throw a bunch of individual values enclosed in parentheses, as an assignment to a val, and a tuple is formed, whose field types are inferred from those values.

scala> val t = (1, "abc", 20.0)
t: (Int, String, Double) = (1, abc, 20.0)

And you just access the individual fields by ._<n> where n is the number of field starting with 1

scala> println("The id is " + t._1 + " and the name is " + t._2)
The id is 1 and the name is abc

You could work with a structure like account using a tuple, instead of a class (unless you needed explicit naming of fields etc.).

scala> val acct1 = (12, 25.50)
acct1: (Int, Double) = (12, 25.5)

A tuple could be multi dimensional (i.e. nested)

scala> type row = (Int, Int)
defined type alias row

scala> type matrix2x2 = (row, row)
defined type alias matrix2x2

scala> val m: matrix2x2 = ((1, 2), (2, 4))
m: matrix2x2 = ((1, 2), (2, 4))

scala> val a12 = m._1._2
a12: Int = 2

Few functional tricks

Default parameters
Functions can take default parameters (like class construction).

So you can define a function multiply -

*scala> def multiply(a: Int, b: Int = 2) = a * b*
multiply: (a: Int, b: Int)Int

with a default value for the second argument. If you provide two parameters during the call, it will make use of both -

scala> val x = multiply(3, 5)
x: Int = 15

Supply only one, and that would be taken in place of the first argument, and will be multiplied with the default value for the second argument (which is 2).

scala> val y = multiply(4)
y: Int = 8

Multiple parameter set
Scala functions can take more than one set of parameters. e.g. -

scala> def sumoffour(a:Int, b:Int)(c:Int, d:Int) = a + b + c + d
sumoffour: (a: Int, b: Int)(c: Int, d: Int)Int

scala> val n = sumoffour(1,2)(3,4)
n: Int = 10

...

Type inference for a later set of parameters is possible in an invocation, with earlier parameter values provided.

scala> def myop[A,B](x: A)(y: B)(op : (A,B) => B) = op(x,y)
myop: [A, B](x: A)(y: B)(op: (A, B) => B)B

*scala> val z = myop(1)(2.5)((x,y) => x * y)*
z: Double = 2.5

Implicit parameters

In Scala, functions can take implicit parameters. Which means those parameter(s) need not be explicitly provided while calling the function - so long as an implicit value of the same type is available in scope.

If you put the following code in a file -

implicit val x:Int = 2

*def multiple(a: Int)(implicit b:Int) = a * b*

println ("result is " + multiple(3))

and run it, it should produce

result is 6

The second parameter (the last set of parameter(s)) is not supplied on function call, but an implicit val of type Int is defined in scope. Hence this implicit value is taken. If the function was called with multiple(3)(4) [i.e. providing the parameter explicitly as 4], that would have resulted in the value 12.

Note that *implicit* applies to a whole set of parameters. So if you want to apply it to a single parameter, that parameter should be segregated in a parameter set by itself.

Note how the following definition is interpreted as implicit for both b and c.

*scala> def multi(a: Int)(implicit b:Int, c:Float) = a * b*

multi: (a: Int)(implicit b: Int, implicit c: Float)Int

And the following does not compile.

scala> def abc(a:Int, implicit b:Float) = "dummy"

<console>:1: error: identifier expected but 'implicit' found.

...

by-name parameters

Usually arguments in a Scala function are passed by-value. i.e. they are evaluated prior to the function call. For example -

scala> def x(a:Int) = { println("evaluating x"); a * 1}

x: (a: Int)Int

scala> def y(a:Int) = { println("evaluating y"); a * 2}

y: (a: Int)Int

scala> def sum(m:Int, n:Int) = { println("by value " + (m + m + n + n)) }

sum: (m: Int, n: Int)Unit

scala> def sum2(m: => Int, n: => Int) = { println("by name " + (m + m + n + n)) }

sum2: (m: => Int, n: => Int)Unit

scala> val z1 = sum(x(1),y(1))

evaluating x

evaluating y

by value 6

z1: Unit = ()

scala> val z2 = sum2(x(1),y(1))

evaluating x

evaluating x

evaluating y

evaluating y

by name 6

z2: Unit = ()

The function sum takes it's arguments by-value. Hence the arguments are evaluated (by evaluating the functions x and y, with their respective arguments [i.e. x(1) and y(1)]) prior to execution of the function body of sum. (As is evident from the print messages).

On the other hand, the function sum2 takes both it's arguments by-name (putting => prior to the Int type), and hence those parameters are evaluated as and when each of the values are used in the function (and not prior to starting the function body of sum2).

Perhaps it will be more evident with the following definition of sum2.

scala> def sum2(m: => Int, n: => Int) = { val a = m + m

| println("in the middle")

| val b = a + n + n

| println("b = " + b) }

sum2: (m: => Int, n: => Int)Unit

scala> val z3 = sum2(x(1),y(1))

evaluating x

evaluating x

in the middle

evaluating y

evaluating y

b = 6

z3: Unit = ()

Note that (1) this business of by-name and by-value does not apply to the whole function, rather it is more about individual parameters. In a function each of the parameters could be passed (rather evaluated in way of) either by-name or by-value (based on the type definition of the parameter having => preceding the other type [e.g. => Int vs Int]).

(2)   'Int' and '=> Int' are not the same types. '=> int' is a *type which is 'a function that will generate an Int value'.*

So (a) when a function (say hof1) expects an Int argument –

def hof1(a: Int) ...

if you pass to it a function call instead (which after evaluation will return an Int) – like

hof1(multplyBy2(3))

it will first completely evaluate the inner function, get the resultant Int value as it's input, and then proceed to do it's own business.

Whereas (b) if you have a function (say hof2) which takes an '=> Int' as an argument,

def hof2(a: => Int) ...

if you pass to it a function call, which after evaluation
returns an Int, like -

hof2(multplyBy2(3))

it will (in a manner of speaking) take it at the right spirit of –
"my argument is 'a function that returns an Int'" and not as "my
argument is an Int", and proceed to do it's business in general,
knowing that it has a function - ready to be called, at it's disposal,
which will return an Int – and call it (if and) only when it is required
to do so.

Note the code run (below) -

scala> def multiplyBy2(a:Int) = {

  | println("multiplying by 2")

  | a * 2

  | }

multiplyBy2: (a: Int)Int

scala> def hof2(a: => Int): Int = {

  | val calling = false

  | if (calling) a

  | else 1

  | }

hof2: (a: => Int)Int

scala> val x = hof2(multiplyBy2(3))

x: Int = 1

the function *hof2*, is specifically rigged not to actually

make use of *multiplyBy2*. And it didn't. (If it did the *println* from the function multiplyBy2 would have been executed.)

Lazy and eager evaluation of functions

def, val and lazy val

There are subtle differences in evaluation of values. When you define something with the *def* keyword, it is evaluated when it is called (and every time it is called, and not evaluated if it is never called). When you define something with the *val* keyword, it is evaluated once at definition (even if it is never used), and not thereafter.

So def leads to lazy evaluation, and val leads to eager evaluation. Each of them have their advantages and disadvantages. One simple case in point is that, if you want a function which (say) generates a random integer value between 1 and 20, if you define it with *val*, you will get the same value for the variable in multiple places in your program. Whereas def will mean it is evaluated every time it is called and hence you will most likely end up with different values at different places (unless by chance some or all values happen to be calculated the same, even on multiple invocation of random Int generation).

You can additionally define a value as *lazy val* instead of *val*. This will make it evaluate lazily (like def) but only once (on first invocation).

scala> import scala.util.Random

import scala.util.Random

scala> def x = Random.nextInt(10) // value between 0 and 9

x: Int

71

scala> val y = Random.nextInt(10)

y: Int = 5

scala> lazy val z = Random.nextInt(10)

z: Int = <lazy>

scala> val a = 2 * z //first incovation of lazy val

a: Int = 8

scala> val b = x * 2

b: Int = 0

scala> val c = 3 * z //z should be 4 as per first invocation

c: Int = 12

scala> val d = x * 2

d: Int = 18

Note that lazy val can be a good way of 'memoizing' the result of a complicated calculation once and for all, and use the result in multiple places.

Derived functions

Given one or more functions, it is possible to derive other functions from those. [it is more like tweaking around with parameter arrangement, output, invocation, etc., rather than touching the actual processing or calculation that the function meant to accomplish]. Such derived functions may be easier to use in some context, than the original functions.

Tupled

If you have a function which has an input parameter signature of certain type [say (Int, String, Int)], and you have a tuple with the same signature - you can pass the tuple to a function created by calling *tupled* on the original function value (rather than extracting values from the tuple, and then passing it to original function).

scala> val f1 = (x:Int, y:String, z:Int) => println("The " + y + " is " + (x + z))
f1: (Int, String, Int) => Unit = <function3>

scala> val f2 = f1.tupled
f2: ((Int, String, Int)) => Unit = <function1>

scala> f1(2, "sum", 3)
The sum is 5

scala> val t = (4, "addition of 4 and 5", 5)
t: (Int, String, Int) = (4, addition of 4 and 5, 5)

scala> f2(t)
The addition of 4 and 5 is 9

Partially applied functions

If you have a plain *multiply* function in the scope, like -

*def multiply(a: Int, b: Int) = a * b*

and for your purpose, you are sure that you are only ever going to multiply anything by 2, then you can apply the function partially to create another function, that just needs one argument , (the number that you are going to double).

```scala
scala> def doubleIt(a:Int) = multiply(a, 2)
doubleIt: (a: Int)Int
```

```scala
scala> val z = doubleIt(7)
z: Int = 14
```

Similar effect can be achieved using placeholder syntax.

```scala
scala> def doub = multiply(_:Int, 2)
doub: Int => Int
```

```scala
scala> val w = doub(7)
w: Int = 14
```

Currying

Sometimes it is convenient (especially in functional programming) to convert a flat function, which takes a single set of (multiple) parameters, to a nested higher order function, created by successive right nesting of the input and output argument type set of the original function. Hopefully it will be clearer in demonstration.

```scala
scala> val f1 = (a:Int, b:Float, c:String) => println(c + " is " + (a + b))
f1: (Int, Float, String) => Unit = <function3>
```

```scala
scala> val f2 = f1.curried
f2: Int => (Float => (String => Unit)) = <function1>
```

Here the function taking an argument set (Int, Float, String) and with output type Unit (i.e. (Int, Float, String) => Unit), is converted [by calling *curried* on the function value] to a function, which takes an Int (the leftmost input argument type of the original function value), and providing an output type, which in turn is another function of type *Float => (String => Unit)*

To see it's usage (in a rather simplistic way) -

scala> f1(1, 2.5f, "sum")

sum is 3.5

scala> val x = f2(1)

x: Float => (String => Unit) = <function1>

scala> val y = x(2.5f)

y: String => Unit = <function1>

scala> y("sum")

sum is 3.5

It allows you to convert a simple function to an HOF with multi level nesting, and it would be possibly to apply the parameters at different stages in the overall processing. Think of an assembly line, where in one shop, some half finished product comes in, and the workers there are responsible to attach, just another extra part to the half finished assembly, and then pass it on to the next shop in the line.

Currying is named after Haskell Curry (an American mathematician) and has nothing to do with curry in the cooking sense. It is in a way the process of breaking down a normal multi- parameter function to a chain of partially applied functions.

In my opinion, it is really a way of deriving an HOF (of a particular form), from a given function - in order to use it more suitably in a context (that requires step by step partial application of the original parameters). However, as I understand, it is widely recognized as a way of dependency injection. An example will probably make it easier to understand.

Suppose you have a function, which generates invitation letters to some recipients, given the venue, the occasion and name of the recipient. (Without going into too much of a fancy format, let's restrict our letter to only 3 lines of text).

```
def letter(venue: String, occasion: String, name: String) : Unit = {

    println("Dear " + name)

    println("You are cordially invited to " + venue +

        " on the joyous occasion of " + occasion)

    println("Regards")

}
```

```
letter("Wolfenden Hall", "anniversary of our institution", "Roy")
```

Upon currying the function 'letter' would produce a chain of functions of type String => (String => (String => Unit))

In a given situation, usually both the venue and the occasions would be known. Only the names need to be applied per individual. Hence we can already apply the first two parameters in the chain, and make it a simpler partially applied function, which takes only the name of an individual and can provide the final letter.

```
def letter(venue: String, occasion: String, name: String) : Unit = {
    println("Dear " + name)
    println("You are cordially invited to " + venue +
        " on the joyous occasion of " + occasion)
```

println("Regards")

}

val f1 = letter(_,_,_)
val curriedLetter = f1.curried

val invite = curriedLetter("Wolfenden Hall")("anniversary of our institution")

invite("Roy")

It ultimately produces the same result as before, but now the dependency of venue and occasion having injected, the final function can be called several times - with just different names - to get the desired result.

[If, in your thinking mode, you replace the venue and occasion with values like database, userid and password, and think of name as a query string, you will find, using the same technique, you can create a derived function with database, userid and password injected, and you can call this function with many valid query string, without worrying about the connection part.]

Note that the line,

val f1 = letter(_,_,_)

converts the original function to a function value easily.

scala> val f1 = letter(_,_,_)

f1: (String, String, String) => Unit = <function3>

And that helps creating the curried function easily (saves some typing), without explicitly defining the function type of the original function.

Uncurrying

Is just the opposite process, which takes a curried function and makes it a simpler multi- parameter function.

val f1 : Int => Int => String => Unit = a => b => c => println(c + " is " + (a + b))

f1(2)(3)("sum")

val f2 = Function.uncurried(f1)

f2(6, 3, "addition")

Should produce

sum is 5
addition is 9

Note that, unlike curried, *uncurried* is not directly called on the function itself, but on the *Function* object.

Note also that a function of type *Int => Int => String => Unit* is a function *that*

takes an Int and returns a function
that takes an Int and returns a function
that takes a String and returns an Unit

Composition of functions

Given two functions, and in a situation where you need to pass the result of the first function call to the second function, to get the final result - you can compose those two given functions into one, by using either *compose* or *andThen*

val incrementIt : Int => Int = a => a + 1

*val doubleIt : Int => Int = b => b * 2*

val incrementAndDouble1 = doubleIt compose incrementIt

println(incrementAndDouble1(5))

val incrementAndDouble2 = incrementIt andThen doubleIt

println(incrementAndDouble2(5))

val doubleAndIncrement = doubleIt andThen incrementIt

println(doubleAndIncrement(5))

produces

12

12

11

Note that *andThen* puts function execution in reversed order compared to *compose*.

...

These are some of the ways, functions can be derived from other given functions, and may be used more suitably in certain contexts.

Traits

Eagle is a class of birds, and so is Crow. In an object oriented world, a particular crow may be modelled by an instance of Crow class. The same could be said about a particular Eagle. But what about birds?

How would you say that something (some animal apparently) is a bird? What makes a bird a bird?

You could start by describing the trait of a bird such as – (a) a bird has wings, (b) a bird can fly (c) a bird has legs with feet suitable for sitting on a perch, and so on. A trait is essentially that. Set of attributes and capabilities that makes something that something (e.g. that makes a bird a bird). [Note that you could possibly say the same thing about a class definition also – i.e. what makes an eagle an eagle. (and in a sense it is perhaps true for any reference template). However – a trait is a higher level (or more general) abstraction, than classes, as it abstracts over classes in some sense]

Syntactically, in Scala, (somewhat like an interface in Java) a trait is a reference template that has attributes (fields) and capabilities (methods). And traits can be mixed in (or more familiarly extended by) classes.

...

For example suppose you want to abstract over some classes, that has a *name* and an *age*. You want to generalise anything that has a *name* and an *age*, and define it as a trait. Let's name the trait as *HasNameAndAge*.

What could be some example classes, that should have this *trait*. It could for instance be a *Person*, a *Student*, a *Customer* and so on. Although those particular classes may model the behaviour for a wider variety of functions, *each of them could share the trait, that they have a name and an age.*

How would the syntax look like ? See the example code below -

```
trait HasNameAndAge {
        val name = "Default"
        val age = 20


        def isValidAge(): Boolean =
                if ((age < 0) || (age > 150)) false else true
}


class Person(name: String, age: Int) extends HasNameAndAge
val p1 = new Person("Arian", 35)
```

println("Age of Arian is valid ? " + p1.isValidAge)

    In the above trait, apart from the attributes *name* and *age*, the trait also has a validation method for age (that it should be within a range). When the class *Person* extends it, it inherits the method also.

    If the code is run, it should result in the following being printed in console -

Age of Arian is valid ? True

    ...

    After some basic Scala, let's turn our attention to recursion.

Recursive functions

"To understand recursion, one must first understand recursion."
- Stephen Hawking

Recursive functions are functions that, in short – *calls itself* (hence the name). In a slightly more detail – a recursive function calls itself at least once (somewhere in it's definition).

A few other facts to note is that -

(1) The call within the function body (almost invariably) should not happen using the exact same parameter value of the function call [Otherwise it would almost inevitably get into an infinite loop and possibly crash the system]. The inner call (or calls) should happen, in some sense, with a reduced parameter. (E.g. lesser valued number, or a subset of the original array and so on). What parameter value the next level (the inner call) will recur with, should be based on the *stepping of the recursion*. (This will hopefully be evident in our first example).

(2) There has to be a limiting parameter value (at least one), encountering which, the function will stop recursion. [Not call itself if that is the parameter value. Instead it can return a predefined value, or take an alternate path and so on]. Let's call it *stopping of the recursion* (somewhat in keeping with the earlier *stepping of the recursion*).

Note that both *stepping* and *stopping*, may have multiple occurrence in a function (almost invariably with mutually different parameters)

(3) Quite often, but not always, a recursive function may do things other than either stepping or stopping. For instance –

(a) In presence of an invalid parameter, which is neither the stop signal, nor fit to be further recursed with [i.e. neither fit for stepping, nor fit for stopping]. (For example – take a function which is defined only for non-negative integer, and where stopping signal is 0, and stepping signal is any positive integer. If this is passed a negative integer, it has to throw an exception. You may choose not to do anything also, but in any case this should not go down the path of either stepping or stopping).

(b) It may do other calculations as part of it's process, before invoking the next step (in view of the overall deliverable)

Let's call the third type as *laterality of the recursion*.

Stepping, stopping and *laterality* are the cornerstones of recursive functions.

...

Recursive functions are not exclusive to functional programming. However, a language supporting FP - usually makes the use of recursion more wide spread, and easy – and that gives greater power and choice to the programmer. With that power and choice, an experienced functional thinker may naturally tend to think of using recursion in a solution - which lends itself naturally to a recursive way of solution.

The Factorial

One classic example of recursive solution is, calculation of factorial for a non-negative integer.

Factorial of a non-negative integer, can be expressed as -
factorial(0) = 1
factorial(1) = 1
factorial(n) [for n : Integer; n < 0] = n * (n-1) * .... * 3 * 2 * 1

(For negative integers, it is not defined)

...

In order to define such a function recursively – first note the *stepping* and *stopping* conditions.

The *stopping* happens when the input value is either 0 or 1. In either case it should return 1.

The *stepping* is simply calling the function with a value, which is 1 less than the original parameter value (i.e. $n - 1$).

There is also the validation (for non-negative) involved, which is the *laterality* in this case.

In a pseudo-code way – it could be something like

```
factorial(n) = {
    if (n < 0) throw exception
    if (n == 0 or n == 1) 1
    else n * factorial(n-1)
}
```

When the inner call materialises, what was originally $n - 1$ becomes n for the new (next level) of recursion. But since the result of inner call has been multiplied with (original) n – it would produce correct result.

(Assuming we started with a positive integer greater than 1), at one point, the n-1 of inner call (the n of the next level) will assume the value of 1, and the function will enter the stop condition (the if part rather than the else) - and will return the fixed value 1, rather than calling itself again. This will start the chain reaction of multiplication of the stacked values [and here I am using the word stack in it's simple english sense rather than computer language sense] in the opposite direction, and finally yield the result.

A more detailed walkthrough with a specific parameter value (say 4), when completely unfolded will look like -

4 * (result of factorial(3) which is 3 *

(result of factorial(2) which is 2 *
    (result of factorial(1) which is 1)
or more simply – (4 * 3 * 2 * 1)

A simple definition in Scala, of the same function, does not look much more different than the pseudo-code discussed earlier.

If you put the following code in a file named *factorial.scala -*

```
def factorial(n: Int): Int = {

  if (n < 0)

    throw new IllegalArgumentException("Not defined [negative integer].");

  else if ((n == 0) || (n == 1)) 1

  else n * factorial(n-1)

}


println

println("factorial(0) : " + factorial(0))

println("factorial(4) : " + factorial(4))

print("factorial(-4) : ")

factorial(-4)
```

And try to run it in REPL using ':load factorial.scala' from same directory, you should get something like -

```
scala> :load factorial.scala

Loading factorial.scala...

factorial: (n: Int)Int
```

factorial(0) : 1

factorial(4) : 24

factorial(-4) : java.lang.IllegalArgumentException: Not defined [negative integer].

 at .factorial(<console>:14)

 ... 55 elided

Crux of recursion stepping

When a recursive step is happening monotonically, being dependent only on (one) current and (one) next value, (such as in factorial), it is easier to conceive. However things get complicated when more parameters, or more than one step-state is involved. A good example of more than one step-state - is Fibonacci sequence. [step-state is the states (or particular argument values) - required for a particular step. (basically the value of argument set for that step). They are being called step-state to emphasise the fact that the states (argument values), changes from step to step]

A *Fibonacci sequence* is an integer sequence which starts with two starting numbers (which is usually 1,1, but sometimes taken as 0,1 also) and thereafter each number in the sequence is the sum of previous two numbers. Thus -

either : 1, 1, 2, 3, 5, 8, 13, 21, ...

or : 0, 1, 1, 2, 3, 5, 8, 13, 21, ...

Note that except for the extra 0 in front, the above two are the same sequence.

...

Think of a single step of recursion in the middle. You have

86

(k-2)th term [say a] and *(k-1)th* term (say b). Clearly for this step the function should take *a*, and *b*, as input and provide c (= a+b) as the *kth* term. But what is it going to pass to the next step. b and c right ? So this is a function which takes in *a* and *b* as parameters, returns c as part of the result [this term] and calls itself with *b* and c – right? Try thinking of formulating such a function.

There are actually two complexity involved here. (Apparent) multiplicity of parameters, and interdependence of parameters. (Apparent) multiplicity, because each step seem to require two parameters, and interdependence, because the second parameter (b) is not fully independent of the first parameter (a). *b* was calculated in a previous step, using *a* as one of the arguments.

...

In designing solution for this kind of recursion, (in my opinion) you would first need to think of stepping. [*In fact that is perhaps true for any type of recursion. Stopping and laterality are usually more obvious and less tricky than stepping – and quite often can be derived as a by product of stepping design*] In order to design for the stepping, it is good advice to -

1)   First of all focus on a single step in the middle.

2)   Think of complete set of input and output states for this step, from the point of view of the overall series of results. (not from the point of view of the function).

3)   Separate the input set as one set, and the output set as another set. [step-state for current step, and step-state for next step] (from the point of view of the function).

4)   Weave in the interdependency (amongst parameters, and if necessary with output values of the step also).

May be a concrete example would help.

(1) In the middle of the series take a trio : a, b, c [This is as things are from the overall series's perspective] .

At this step the function should take in *a* and *b,* and produce *c.* [From the functions perspective].

But note that the input set is (a,b) but output set is not just c. If you think of *what you are handing to the next step* (call it *next step-state*) you actually need to handover both b and c [otherwise how will the next step do it's work ?]

So you really should take in (a, b) [complete input set] and produce (b,c) [complete output set].

Now weave the interdependency. We know that c is a + b. *As far as a, b, and c goes, that is the only interdependence we can materialise fully for this step. b* is dependent on *a,* but that dependence can not be fully formulated, without going past *a* (backwards – i.e. without looking at things previous to *a*).

So we are taking in (a,b) and giving out (b, a+b) [for next step of recursion].

Our preliminary function design then is (in pseudo-code) -

```
f (a: Int, b: Int) = {

    ...

    f (b, a+ b)

}
```

So in some sense we have captured the crux of recursion step-state. And that (in my opinion) is the heart of this recursion problem. (The rest in a way is by product).

...

So, we know how to step [*stepping of recursion*]. Now only two other things – (*stopping of recursion*) when to stop ?, and if there is any *laterality of recursion,* (i.e. what other things are to be done - towards the end deliverable ?)

...

Stopping of recursion : Stopping of recursion for such a function, would be a boundary value given at the top level. i.e. you would usually have a function like -

fibonacciSequence(n: Int): List[Int]

where you specify the nth term, up to which you want the series. So here the *terminating condition* (as in many other cases) *comes from the input to the top level function.*

Laterality of recursion : Laterality of recursion here, (as in many other cases you would probably notice in due course), *comes from the requirement of the end deliverable.*

Designing for final deliverable : Taking of final deliverable - at some point (actually when you have hit the terminating condition), your application will demand that you produce the whole output. Hence you need to stack up the results of calculation from each step, into a series, which you finally can deliver.

Note that in a sense, c is the real product of this step. You already was given a and b. So you need to push c into an accumulation stack, which can finally be used to deliver the result. [Here stack is meant as a general term – just to denote the accumulated result, and not in data structure definition terms.]

Since this accumulation stack needs to be (finally) delivered - it needs to be (a) either a global stack, from the perspective of a step function, or (b) has to be passed on from step to step, each step potentially adding a member to the stack. Note that the same applies to the boundary value (value for terminating condition). It has to be (a) either global to the step function or (b) passed as an input to the step function.

We also need to keep track of the current term (e.g. *k* of the *kth* term), so that the step function can decide when to stop

...

So considering both *accumulation* and termination (*stopping*), (on top of our earlier consideration of *stepping*), our second level refinement of earlier function design should become (in pseudo-code) -

f (a: Int, b: Int, k: Int, n:Int, acc: List[Int]) = {

  if (k > n) return acc // the accumulated result

  else {

   c = a +b

   acc += c //push to stack

   k = k + 1 //increase the term by one

   f (b, a+ b, k, n, acc) // k and acc have both changed

  }

 }

Note that this is the variety where we are taking the option of passing the accumulation and condition. (just as a reminder, the other option is global stack, and global state for term count (k)).

...

Now formalising this in actual code ,we have the internal function as -

def go (a: Int, b: Int, k: Int, n:Int, acc: ListBuffer[Int]) : ListBuffer[Int] = {

```
if ( k > n) return acc // the accumulated result
else {
        val c = a + b
        acc += c //push to stack
        go (b, a + b, k + 1, n, acc) // k and acc have both
changed
    }
}
```

Note : Increment of k has been pushed into the inner call. Also you need to import ListBuffer for this to work.

...

Now let us look at the starting condition (or *initial step-state*).

When we start (i.e. for the first term to be calculated, we have a and b as 1 and 1 respectively (*we can not calculate the first two terms, because we need two preceding terms to calculate, which is not present for the first two terms*). So for the first calculated term (k = 1), which is actual the 3rd number in the sequence, *a* and *b* are 1 and 1 respectively. So if we want the terms calculated up to the 4th term (n = 4) starting from the first calculable term (which is the 3rd number in the series) we can call this function with a = 1, b = 1, k = 1, n = 4, and the stack (in which accumulation will take place) is as of now empty. Nothing is accumulated yet. so *acc* is an empty ListBuffer. It all comes together in a script like -

import scala.collection.mutable.ListBuffer

def go (a: Int, b: Int, k: Int, n:Int, acc: ListBuffer[Int]) :
ListBuffer[Int] = {

```
if ( k > n) return acc // the accumulated result
    else {
  val c = a + b
  acc += c //push to stack
  go (b, a + b, k + 1, n, acc) // k and acc have both changed
    }
}
```

```
println(go(1, 1, 1, 4, ListBuffer[Int]()).toList)
```

Which when run, produces

```
List(2, 3, 5, 8)
```

...

This is slightly unwieldy. Firstly because you would like to have the whole list (including the initial 1 and 1, which is not being output here). Besides you want a function which – *gives you a list containing the fibonacci sequence up to (and including) nth term.* Which implies you want *a function which takes in an Int argument n, and returns a List of Int containing that many numbers of the sequence from the beginning* (and eventually in that order).

So you are after a function *fib(n: Int) : List[Int]* where the returned list should contain n numbers (not n + 2) and you would not have to know what the series starts with.

...

We can adopt the inner function we designed, by putting it as an inner function to the function you want, like this -

import scala.collection.mutable.ListBuffer

```
def fib(n: Int) : List[Int] = {


    def go (a: Int, b: Int, k: Int, n:Int, acc: ListBuffer[Int]) :
    ListBuffer[Int] = {
            if ( k > n) return acc // the accumulated result
            else {
                    val c = a + b
                    acc += c //push to stack
                    go (b, a + b, k + 1, n, acc) // k and acc have
both changed
            }
    }


    val m = n - 2
    val acc = ListBuffer[Int](1,1)


    val accBuf = go(1, 1, 1, m, acc)
    accBuf.toList
}


println(fib(4))
```

Note that : n has been reduced by 2 to accommodate the first two terms. And those two terms are also put into acc two start with (so that final ListBuffer is returned along with those two terms).

When run it produces -

List(1, 1, 2, 3)

...

it would be possible to not have the terminating condition passed as parameter to the inner function, and use the *val* directly from the outer function. The function then would take the form -

```
def fib(n: Int) : List[Int] = {


    val m = n - 2


    def go (a: Int, b: Int, k: Int, acc: ListBuffer[Int]) :
ListBuffer[Int] = {
        if ( k > m) return acc // the accumulated result
            else {
            val c = a + b
            acc += c //push to stack
            go (b, a + b, k + 1, acc) // k and acc have both
changed
            }
        }


    val acc = ListBuffer[Int](1,1)


    val accBuf = go(1, 1, 1, acc)
    accBuf.toList
```

}

Note that – in this case, the val m have to be defined before the inner function definition. Otherwise it would result in forward reference error.

Note that global stack is not very useful here, because – (1) In Scala a recursive function must return something (so can as well return the accumulated list), (b) the global stack has to be a var (which does not align well with immutability).

In general the first form, where all requisite parameters are passed to the inner function, is more functional than the later form. Referencing values outside the inner function is not very healthy from the referential transparency point of view. The inner function in this case, is not a pure function, as it depends on external state (m).

Tail recursion

If a function is defined such that - after the next level recursion is calculated and returned, you still need to do some work / operation, then the other operand(s) of the operation (other than the result of the next level recursion) has to stacked for the operation to take place.

For example – if a function is defined as (pseudo-code) -

f(n) = n * f (n-1)

[this is more or less factorial without the negative int argument check] then at any level of n, n needs to be kept in store (stack) to carry out the multiplication after f(n-1) returns it's result.

To expand it a bit more, if we start with n = 5 [and assume f(0) = 1] then the various stages of expansion would look like this -

$f(5) = 5 * f(4)$

$f(4) = 4 * f(3)$

...

Which could be thought of as

$f(5) = 5 * (4 * (3 * (2 * (1 * f(0)))))$

The whole thing can be wrapped up only after f(0) has been returned (and then multiplication in reverse order has to take place [based on the nesting parentheses]). Hence all the n's 5,4,3, .. have to be stacked for the final reverse order multiplications to take place.

This kind of recursion is prone to stack overflow error for sufficiently large level of recursions.

Is there a way to avoid this?

A better way would be, when there is are no value(s) to be stacked. - i.e. there is no operation needed after the return of the next level recursion (hence no other side operand - to be stacked). I.e. the last step of the recursion, consists only of the call to next level of recursion, and nothing else.

This kind of recursive call, where the last step of recursion (*last step hence 'tail'*) – is the unmixed call to the next level of recursion (*unmixed – no other operation, purely the call to next step of recursion*), is known as *tail recursion (or tail-call recursion)*. Tail recursions are inherently safe from stack overflow.

Note that the tail position could refer to any of the alternative path of program execution, so long as it is the last possible step in the path [i.e. going down the path, there is nothing else being executed in the function after this step]. So a function can have multiple tails (!) and any of the tail position can do something other than calling the next level recursion (e.g. returning a fixed value) and that is ok. But so long as even one tail, with recursion call, is not unmixed – it is not a tail recursion. (The function as a whole, fails to be tail recursive).

Coming back to the previous example – if the function f(n) were to be modified - to take multiplication operand of the the immediately previous step - as an argument, instead of putting it on stack - then the tail position can have an unmixed call. i.e.

f(currnum, sofar) =

>> *if (currnum == 0)*

>>> *sofar*

>> *else*

>>> *f((currnum - 1), sofar * currnum)*

and hence it need not make use of the stack the way it previously did.

So the key here is *take operand as argument – rather than stacking it.*

...

Eventually it is a good idea to make a recursive function - tail recursive (unless you have a compelling case to do otherwise). However, especially for a large function, it is possible that you wrote the function thinking it is tail recursive, but it is in fact, not. Scala provides a way to verify this assumption at compile time.

You can annotate a function definition, by putting an @annotation.tailrec (see below)

@annotation.tailrec

def facto(n: Int): Int = {

> *if (n == 0) 1*

```
else n * facto(n-1)
}
println("facto(4) : " + facto(4))
```

What it does is that – if a function is not tail recursive, it does not compile. [On the other hand, without the annotation, a non tail-recursive function would compile and be designed to execute using the stack – while you may be on the impression that it has been compiled to be tail recursive]

If you try to run the above code it would produce some thing like -

tailfacto.scala:4: error: could not optimize @tailrec annotated method facto: it contains a recursive call not in tail position

```
else n * facto(n-1)
```

    ^

one error found

On the other hand a proper tail-recursive function, when thus annotated, will not produce such error.

```
@annotation.tailrec
def tailfacto(n: Int, facto:Int): Int = {
  if (n == 0) facto
  else tailfacto(n-1, n * facto)
}
println("tailfacto(4, 1) : " + tailfacto(4, 1))
```

produces

tailfacto(4, 1) : 24

Binary search algorithm

I would like to discuss another well known algorithm, which is amenable to recursion. *Binary search algorithm.*

Binary search algorithm is like the 'poster boy' of algorithms, and if you are a serious programmer, chance is that you have come across it more than once.

However in my view this is an elusively complex algorithm. I am not talking of genius category people, but even for a reasonably good programmer it could be so. When you start to think of it, it may feel deceptively simple, but can soon escalate in complexity, especially when you lax your vigil on structured thinking about the solution.

I would like to walk through the solution steps, prior to presenting the actual code. But before that, let me discuss the basic concept of the algorithm [which works on a linear collection, which is sorted and in some way indexed -e.g. sorted *Array* or *List*.]

Suppose your friend Oscar has asked you to look through the university gazette, to find his yearly Grade Point Average and let him know the same. (He might have planned to busy himself with something else, or could not somehow handle the mental pressure of facing it, and relied upon you to look it up for him.)

The published result is alphabetically sorted on the first name. e.g.

Aaron, 8.5

Albert, 7.8

Alex, 6.4

...

Zelda, 8.9

Zoran, 6.8

Zubin, 5.9

If you have no idea approximately where in the list the name Oscar should be - you could start by looking more or less in the middle of the list, and see the name there. If you find the name is above Oscar in alphabetical order (such as Peter), look through the list below that middle [below meaning the part lesser in alphabetical order than Peter] (and even in this part, first target the middle of it). And so it goes, choosing the right part of the list and sub list to look at unless -

(a) you find his name at the very place you are looking

(b) you zero in on only one name.

If on the other hand the name appears to be below Oscar in alphabetical order on the first look , (such as Michael), continue your search in the upper part (alphabetically), of the list (and apply the same strategy of halving the list every time).

At any point you may find his name at the very place where you are looking, and your search is over. On the other hand if you narrow down your searchable domain, down to one name only, and that is not his name, and (in a manner of speaking) you are out of luck (or perhaps Oscar is). In that case his GPA is not found in the list (but your search is concluded in any case).

In binary search algorithm, it is the same principle (except that you look exactly in the middle). More precisely -

(1) Look at the middle item of the list

(2a) If it is the target item return the required value

(2b) If it is an item ahead of the target item, make the lower half of the list (excluding this item) your new domain of search and look there [i.e. go to step (1) with the reduced domain]

(2c) If it is an item behind the target item, make the upper half of the list (excluding this item) your new domain for search and look there [i.e. go to step (1) with the reduced domain]

So it involves -

(a) Finding the middle item of the current scope

(b) look up the indicator value at that element, and match it against the target value. [In this example case, the *indicator value* is the *name*, and the target value is *Oscar* (and the *required value to be delivered* is the GPA – once the target value is found)].

This looking is not binary. You will need to decide whether it is the target, or it is above the target or below the target. So one of three possible values.

(c) based on the returned value of comparison from (b), change your scope - [original start to original mid – 1] or [original mid + 1 to original end], and go back to step (a) above [or call the search function recursively] with new scope.

Clear ?

Well, the first slight hitch is - what is the middle index? It is ok if you have an odd number of items. If the number of items are $2n + 1$, you look at $(n+1)$th item. But what if it is an even number of items? Say 4 items. Will you choose the second or the third item as the middle? Perhaps does not matter much so long as you choose either the second or the third (i.e. either nth or $(n+1)$th for $2n$ number of items) [but keep choosing one or the other consistently, so long as the list to be divided is even numbered].

Also note that the index is zero based (so the first element is with index 0) and even in the sub-divisions, you will need to find an item through it's original index number. (The index position it has in the overall array).

Given the start index of a scope = start, and the end index of a scope = end, one simple formula for finding the middle index position in the scope would be -

mid = start + (end − start + 1) / 2

It relies on integer division to return an integer index – whether or not the scope has odd or even length. [So it works both for either even or odd numbered List]. Note that - for a scope of length 4, it chooses the 3rd item as the mid one [so going the *(n+1)th* way for *2n* items].

...

The comparison, and subsequent returning of one of three possible values (e.g. -1, 0 or 1) - should be fairly straightforward. [I chose -1 as an indication that we need to look at the lower half, a matter of convention really.]

So given a scope (or range of items), you find the mid item and compare the indicator value with the target value.

Once the result of comparison is zero you are done. But if it is -

-1 => scope it to start to mid -1 (and recurse)

1 => scope it to mid + 1 to end (and recurse)

...

But the above is about a range. What if you are down to one element (the scope itself has reduced to one element) ? Sub-division is meaningless here. At this point, just look at the element, if you got what you are looking for, return the required value, otherwise give up.

Clear now ?

...

The example I have chosen for coding this algorithm, is actually a small array of strings, where each element is a comma separated Country name and corresponding capital. Somewhat like -

"Afghanistan,Kabul",

"Albania,Tirana",

"Argentina,Buenos Aires",

"Barbados,Bridgetown",

...

The task is - given this list and given a country - find out it's capital using the algorithm.

On internet or elsewhere, you may find working code for this algorithm, which is much shorter (than translating what I have described above). However I wanted to point out that the algorithm has finer points, which are perhaps not so simple. But more importantly I wanted to break it down to – *stepping, stopping, and laterality* paradigm of recursion that I talked about earlier. If you have identified these three aspects of a recursion, the recursion is won over. [And keeping with this paradigm, my solution presented here will be somewhat lengthy – and somewhat of a translation of what I have described above – with a lot of comments interjected. [*People who are experts, (and who actually understood the essence of the algorithm in enough detail) by all means are free to use a short and elegant solution (I am hoping it is not just short it is elegant too. Otherwise ...)*]. But I would suggest - understanding (and 'winning over') an algorithm is more basic requirement than shortness of code.

As an aside – space/memory efficiency, and computational

performance also come before shortness of code. If you recall our earlier example – the tail-recursive solution for factorial, would be lengthier (in terms of number of characters) than the non tail-recursive one, if someone sticks to the same convention of variable and function naming. (And I am not elaborating on somebody else taking over the maintenance of the code from the developer. Although I should add, even lengthy code can be written in a very complicated manner, and when that happens, it leads to 'more fun' - speaking in a rather sarcastic fashion).

...

One other thing, before we embark on the actual code. [*In terms of designing a single step*] at any stage, what all (parameters) do we need, to carry on with the search? We need the original array where to look for, we need the target value (for the indicator) which we are looking for, we also need the scope where we are looking for (which is defined by the start and end index). And the overall code looks like -

val capitals: Array[String] = Array (

"Afghanistan,Kabul",

"Albania,Tirana",

"Argentina,Buenos Aires",

"Barbados,Bridgetown",

"Belarus,Minsk",

"Belgium,Brussels",

"Cambodia,Phnom Penh",

"Cameroon,Yaounde",

"Canada,Ottawa",

"Denmark,Copenhagen",

```scala
    "Dominica,Roseau",
    "Dominican Republic,Santo Domingo",
    "Ecuador,Quito",
    "Egypt,Cairo",
    "El Salvador,San Salvador",
    "Fiji,Suva",
    "Finland,Helsinki",
    "France,Paris",
    "Georgia,Tbilisi",
    "Germany,Berlin"
)


@annotation.tailrec
def binSrch(list: Array[String], lookFor: String)
(implicit start: Int=0, end: Int=list.length-1): String = {

  if (list.isEmpty) {
        return "Could not find. Array is empty."
        //throw new Exception("Empty Array")
  }

  def compare(index: Int, lookFor: String): Int = {
        val country = list(index).split(",")(0)
        println("start, end, mid, country : " +
```

```
                start + ", " + end + ", " + index + ", " + country)
        if (country == lookFor) 0
        else if(country > lookFor) -1
        else 1

    }


    if (start == end) { //[stopping]
            //indices converged - no further division of search domain is
    possible
            //look at the index, if found return, otherwise can't be found
            val rslt = compare(start, lookFor)
            if (rslt == 0) //found, return the required string
                    list(start).split(",")(1)
            else //Not found - and no further search possible
                    "Could not be found"
    } else { //[laterality - explore further]
        //indices not yet converged - look at the middle and
            //if found return, otherwise subdivide the domain, and look
    in the proper sub-division
            val mid = start + (end - start + 1) / 2
            val rslt = compare(mid, lookFor) //look at the middle
            println("rslt : " + rslt)
            if (rslt == 0) // found - return [stopping]
                    list(mid).split(",")(1)
            else if (rslt < 0) //look thorough the lower half [stepping]
```

binSrch(list, lookFor)(start, mid-1)

else //look thorugh the upper half [stepping]

binSrch(list, lookFor)(mid+1, end)

}

}

println("Capital of Finland : " + binSrch(capitals, "Finland"))

println("Capital of Australia : " + binSrch(capitals, "Australia"))

As you can see, it is tail-recursive, and I have clearly indicated the stepping and stopping parts. Also the *compare* function has been added as an inner function. In a different case, you may have to compare different type of things. For instance you could have a list where the first part is an employee id (an Int) and the second part is his or her name. In that case the above recursive function code can be reused in the most part. Largely changing the *compare* function appropriately should do the trick.

I have also left a couple of debug statements (println), which you may wish to comment out for when you need the actual result. But this is just to show how the convergence takes place as the algorithm runs through the array.

Running as it is – it should produce something like -

start, end, mid, country : 0, 19, 10, Dominica

rslt : 1

start, end, mid, country : 11, 19, 15, Fiji

rslt : 1

start, end, mid, country : 16, 19, 18, Georgia

rslt : -1

start, end, mid, country : 16, 17, 17, France

rslt : -1

start, end, mid, country : 16, 16, 16, Finland

Capital of Finland : Helsinki

start, end, mid, country : 0, 19, 10, Dominica

rslt : -1

start, end, mid, country : 0, 9, 5, Belgium

rslt : -1

start, end, mid, country : 0, 4, 2, Argentina

rslt : 1

start, end, mid, country : 3, 4, 4, Belarus

rslt : -1

start, end, mid, country : 3, 3, 3, Barbados

Capital of Australia : Could not be found

    ...

Our present discussion on recursion is hereby concluded.

Pattern matching in Scala

"'Pattern design' is designing of patterns. 'Design pattern' is pattern of design"

Pattern design is Scala is quite powerful and rather ubiquitous. So much so that after getting well enough into Scala, you may find yourself trying to resort to it by default, before considering any other way to solve a problem, in many cases.

The use case for pattern matching is huge in variation. Not all of which will be described in this chapter. Partly considering the length and scope of the book itself. But also because a lot of functional features has not been presented so far (some of which may happen going forward), and hence pattern matching, that involve those features, will be meaningless to discuss now. (For the sake of pattern matching, I may briefly discuss some of those topics in this chapter).

But even so I feel it is a good idea, to present a chapter on the topic, at this point. (Even what can be discussed at this point is lengthy enough and (hopefully) interesting enough. (You might already be familiar with the basic pattern matching of Scala - but still it would be a good idea to browse through the chapter).

Pattern matching with cases

The initial analogy of pattern matching may the the switch statement in many languages (such as in Java), [but that really is too basic an analogy].

The usual form is -

<val / var / expression to be matched> match {

    case <pattern1> => <code to be executed and/or value to be returned, if match is found with pattern1>

    case <pattern2> => <code to be executed and/or value to be returned, if match is found with pattern2>

    ...

    case _ => <code to be executed if none of the above patterns can be matched>

}

    Scala pattern match goes by the first-match policy. Hence catchall kind of matches should be located towards the bottom, otherwise the match could find a very general pattern, rather than a specific one.

Value match
One simple example would be -

val x = 2

val y = x match {

    case 0 => "Zero"

    case 1 => "One"

    case 2 => "Two"

    case 3 => "Three"

    case _ => "None"

}

println(y)

    Which should print

Two

when run.

As you can see, *match* statement (like an *if* statement) can be assigned to a *val*. It can also be used as a function definition.

```scala
def isOdd(x: Int): Boolean = x % 2 match {
    case 0 => false
    case _ => true
}


def evaluate(x: Int): String =
    if (isOdd(x)) x + " is odd" else x + " is even"


println(evaluate(5))
println(evaluate(6))
```

Which produces -

5 is odd

6 is even

As you can see, the entire body of the function isOdd consists of a match statement.

...

The return type from all of the cases need not be the same (*well in a general sense*). When they are different, the overall return type is common type covering the return type of all those cases.

```scala
scala> def abc(x: Int) = x match {
    | case 1 => 1
```

| case 2 => "abc"

|}

abc: (x: Int)Any

It is a good idea to cover the default case. In absence of that, if a value is given which is not covered by any case, it results in a *MatchError* at runtime.

For the function shown above, if a value of 3 is passed as parameter it results in the error.

scala> val y = abc(3)

scala.MatchError: 3 (of class java.lang.Integer)

at .abc(<console>:11)

... 32 elided

By convention, in Scala an underscore (_) as a placeholder (in place of a variable, value, parameter etc.) means - you (the programmer), are not particularly interested in what the value really is. In pattern matching such usages of underscore occur abundantly. Usually such placeholders are either not used going forward (see the default case above), or used only once in the case body. [However note that, where it is used in a case body, the type still needs to be unambiguous]

Expression match

Patterns themselves need not be just values. They could be expression too.

def placement(marks: Int) = marks match {

case x if (0 to 35 contains x) => "Fail"

case x if (36 to 45 contains x) => "3rd division"

case x if (46 to 65 contains x) => "2nd division"

case x if (65 to 80 contains x) => "1st division"

```
        case _ => "distinctions"
}
println(placement(67))
```

produces

1st division

Neither they need to be all of the same type.

```
def abc(x: Any) = x match {
        case 2 => "Two"
        case "a" => "Letter a"
        case _ => "something else"
}
println(abc(2))
```

Type match

Pattern matching not only occurs on values and expressions, it can happen on types also, (and that is where greater varieties come in, and perhaps Scala's greater strength of pattern matching shines through)

```
def abc(x: Any) = x match {
        case a:Int => "an Int"
        case a:String => "a String"
        case _ => "something else"
}
println(abc("a"))
```

produces

a String

Extracting tokens

You can extract, different parts of a string by splitting it on some character(s).

def extract1(email : String) = email.split("@") match {

   case Array(a,b) => println("username : " + a + ", domain : " + b)

   case _ => "Not right format"

}

extract1("John.Doe@hotmail.com")

   produces

username : John.Doe, domain : hotmail.com

And you can read lines from a CSV file (for instance), and extract the tokens that you need, and automatically discard lines that do not conform to the right format.

Suppose you have a file containing comma separated first names and last names of some people (and not all lines are in the right format – see below). And you are interested to extract the last names from the valid lines. Suppose the name of the file is *names.txt*, and it contains -

John,Doe

Meridith,Murdoch

noname

Sanjib,Sen

Sana

Waldo,Nunes

   Then the following code -

import scala.io.Source

```
Source.fromFile("names.txt").getLines.foreach { line =>

      line.split(",") match {

            case Array(firstName, lastName) =>
println(lastName)

            case _ =>

      }

}
```

      would produce -

Doe

Murdoch

Sen

Nunes

You can eventually use regular expressions for extracting tokens too. Suppose you have a file named *trainlog.txt* containing the following text -

2016-05-13 13:56:07.812 Train AX01U actual arrival at STRATHFIELD platform # 01

2016-05-13 13:56:08.652 Special announcement : Delay may be expected due to rain.

2016-05-13 13:56:09.067 All services are running normally on Dale line.

2016-05-13 13:56:09.502 Train AX01U actual arrival at CENTRAL platform # 01

2016-05-13 13:56:09.603 Train AX01U actual arrival at BLACKTOWN platform # 01

2016-05-13 13:56:09.942 Shifting to e-ticket soon.

2016-05-13 13:56:11.574 Train AX02D actual arrival at CENTRAL platform # 02

2016-05-13 13:56:11.732 Special announcement : Suspicious package found at HURSTVILLE station.

Suppose further that you are interested in extracting different tokens from two types of patterns. One is special announcements, and the other is train timings (including train name, station and platform). The following code -

import scala.io.Source

import scala.util.matching.Regex

import java.io.{ PrintWriter, File }

val TimePat = "^(.*) Train (.*) actual.*at (.*) platform # (.*)$".r

val AnnouncePat = "^.*Special announcement : (.*)$".r

val inFile = "trainlog.txt"

val outFile = "tokens.txt"

val writer = new PrintWriter(new File(outFile))

Source.fromFile(inFile).getLines.foreach { line =>

    line match {

        case TimePat(time, train, station, platform) =>

            println ("train : " + train +

                    " station : " + station +

                    " platform : " + platform +

                    " time : " + time)

```
            writer.write(train + ", " + station + ", " +
platform + ", " + time + "\n")

            case AnnouncePat(announcement) =>
println("Announcement : " + announcement)

            case _ =>

    }

}


writer.close
```

Should produce (on the console) -

train : AX01U station : STRATHFIELD platform : 01 time : 2016-05-13 13:56:07.812

Announcement : Delay may be expected due to rain.

train : AX01U station : CENTRAL platform : 01 time : 2016-05-13 13:56:09.502

train : AX01U station : BLACKTOWN platform : 01 time : 2016-05-13 13:56:09.603

train : AX02D station : CENTRAL platform : 02 time : 2016-05-13 13:56:11.574

Announcement : Suspicious package found at HURSTVILLE station.

And the output file 'tokens.txt' should have the timing tokens -

AX01U, STRATHFIELD, 01, 2016-05-13 13:56:07.812

AX01U, CENTRAL, 01, 2016-05-13 13:56:09.502

AX01U, BLACKTOWN, 01, 2016-05-13 13:56:09.603

AX02D, CENTRAL, 02, 2016-05-13 13:56:11.574

Match on cons operator

It is possible to match on cons operator (::) of a List to extract the head (and also handle the case if the List is empty).

```
def sum(list: List[Int]): Int = list match {
  case Nil => 0
  case h :: t => h + sum(t)
}
val lst = List(1,2,3)
println(sum(lst))
```

should produce

```
6
```

This is the recommended form of case match for Lists in general. Note that it can be easily adapted to a List of another type (say List[String]) by using a sensible return value for the Nil case and a sensible operation for the other case. For instance, the following -

```
def sum(list: List[String]): String = list match {
  case Nil => ""
  case h :: t => h + sum(t)
}
val lst = List("a","b","c")
println(sum(lst))
```

would concatenate the strings in the list and produce -

```
abc
```

(More for demonstration purposes) you can match for more than two elements with cons operator. For instance since a List(1,2,3) is equivalent to 1 :: 2 :: 3 :: Nil you can write something like.

```
def sum(list: List[Int]): Int = list match {
    case a :: b :: c :: Nil => a + b + c
}
val lst = List(1, 2, 3)
println(sum(lst))
```

This is not good code (although it will run), and used here for demonstration purposes. It is not generic, and will only work for a list with 3 elements. But in reality a list may not have exactly 3 elements. For instance if you call it with a list of 4 Ints it will result in MatchError at runtime.

Even for a list of 3 elements (as shown above), in the REPL you will get a warning for non exhaustive match.

```
cons.scala:1: warning: match may not be exhaustive.
It would fail on the following inputs: List(_), List(_, _), List(_, _, _
_)
def sum(list: List[Int]): Int = list match {
                                ^
one warning found
6
```

...

For *Streams* the cons operator is #::

```
def sum(strm: Stream[Int]): Int = strm match {
    case Stream() => 0
    case h #:: t => h + sum(t)
}
```

```
val strm = Stream(1,2,3,4)

println(sum(strm))
```

would produce -

10

Match for a Map

Pattern match can be helpful in extracting keys and values from a *Map* structure. The following code is a simple demonstration of the use of pattern match to iterate through a map, containing employee id and their weekly salary, and find the maximum salary.

```
import scala.collection.immutable.Map


val map = Map[Int, Double](

        1 -> 500.00,

        2 -> 950.00,

        3 -> 635.00,

        4 -> 650.00
)


def maxval(map: Map[Int, Double]) = {
   var max = 0.0
        map foreach { elem => elem match { case(k, v) => if (v > max) max = v } }
        max
}
println(maxval(map))
```

Case classes and pattern matching

(Almost) any class in Scala can be defined as a case class by putting the keyword *case* in front of the keyword *class*. e.g.

case class Student(name: String, major: String, year: Int)

Defining a class a case class, comes with a lot of goodies, such as -

1. No need to use the new keyword.

2. Everything is immutable by default

3. Getters automatically defined

4. Decent toString() implementation

5. Compliant equals() and hashCode() implemented by default

6. Comes with default companion object implementation with apply() and unapply() methods.

It is very compliant for use in pattern matching.

I mentioned '(Almost) any class' because there are some restrictions too. Among other things -

1. You can't subclass it.

2. It can not have more than 22 parameters.

Similar way, it is possible to have case objects also.

I suspect the very idea of case classes or case objects - comes from having different cases of a particular trait (i.e. different possible cases of something). For instance suppose you want to return a result from a function, and you think it can go in 3 possible ways, (or rather you want to design it that way) -

(1)   The execution completed successfully, and you

need to return a result which is a Double.

(2)   There was some error in execution, but which was transient (like you could not access a database because of network error – which may not happen if you run after 2 hours. Hence a candidate for rerun).

(3)   It did not complete, but it could not do so - because it does not have sufficient data (e.g. there is no record in the input file, and unless the other side – may be your client organisation, finished their job and writes data to the input file, there is no point in running. But you need to inform them first, and will rerun only after they have confirmed that they have successfully written some records to be processed).

So in each of these cases the handling strategy differs. (and that needs to reflect in the design of the result type). In the first case, you can use it readily. In the second case you need to schedule for rerun. And in the third case you need to inform the other party. [And I have not modelled the case where it failed for other reasons, but this is just for demonstration purposes.]

You can model it as three case classes/objects on a Status trait. Like -

trait Status

case class Result(ret: Double) extends Status

case class TransientError(e: Exception) extends Status

case object DataIssue extends Status

And then depending on the case, return the appropriate status from the function. Something like -

def processIt(fileName: String) : Status = {

//Count the number of lines in the file

if (count ==0) {

```
                DataIssue
        } else {
                //try to get db connection
                if (conn.notAvailable)
                        TransientError(e)
                else {
                        //do the actual calculation
                        Result(ret)
                }
        }
}
```

So these are in a way different possible cases of your Statuses.

Later you may take the return value from this function, whatever it is, and can make use of it using pattern matching (because for different cases you want to handle the result in different ways).

An example with rather trivial processing (just for demonstration) would be -

```
trait Status

case class Result(ret: Double) extends Status

case class TransientError(e: Exception) extends Status

case object DataIssue extends Status


def process(x: Int): Status = {
        if (x < o) Result(1.oo)
```

else if (x == 0) TransientError(new Exception("Dummy
Exception"))

    else DataIssue

}

def handleResult(x: Int) = process(x) match {

    case Result(r) => "Value is " + r

    case TransientError(e) => e.getMessage

    case DataIssue => "No record to process"

}

println(handleResult(-1))

println(handleResult(0))

println(handleResult(1))

which would produce -

Value is 1.0

Dummy Exception

No record to process

    ...

A case class may have more than one parameters. You may not always use all of it's parameters in your handling method - sometimes none at all [Just that the Result matches that case is enough to let you handle the case the right way – e.g. case DataIssue above]. Sometimes you may use all the parameters, or just a few.

Pattern matching can help in all these cases.

Suppose you have been sent a customer data file, which

had incomplete information for some records (of course!). Your junior team member managed to extract the information and give you the information wrapped in appropriate cases. You are interested in the contact information. Particularly email (but you also need at least the first name to address the customer in the email). Which you have for some customers. But for some customers, you have the name and phone numbers instead. (You can still call them and get their emails – a slightly different handling). And for others, you only have names (for which you need to get back to your US office and ask them for correct data on those clients [you need to provide them the list of client names though – and it would rather be small, or else ...]).

For the clients to be reported, you need both their first and last names, but where PhoneNo and email is available, you just need their first names. Also your liaison in the US has informed your junior team member, that some of the clients have already been contacted, and he has marked those cases as Contacted, but still provided the first and last name. Good on him, but you don't need the first name and last name for those customers yourself. But need to pass the whole thing (accumulated in a list, of course) to the accounting(!) department.

Practically you have cases which can be described as -

trait CustomerInfo

case class EmailAvailable(fName: String, lName: String, email: String) extends CustomerInfo

case class PhoneNoAvailable(fName: String, lName: String, phoneNo: String) extends CustomerInfo

case class OnlyName(fName: String, lName:String) extends CustomerInfo

case class Contacted(fName: String, lName:String) extends

CustomerInfo

As for your handling method - based on the things you need in each case, it could look like (putting together with the case classes and import) -

import scala.collection.mutable.ListBuffer

trait CustomerInfo

case class EmailAvailable(fName: String, lName: String, email: String) extends CustomerInfo

case class PhoneNoAvailable(fName: String, lName: String, phoneNo: String) extends CustomerInfo

case class OnlyName(fName: String, lName:String) extends CustomerInfo

case class Contacted(fName: String, lName:String) extends CustomerInfo

def handleCases(infoLst: List[CustomerInfo]) = {

   val emailbuf = ListBuffer[(String, String)]()

   val phonebuf = ListBuffer[(String, String)]()

   val namebuf = ListBuffer[(String, String)]()

   val contactedbuf = ListBuffer[Contacted]()

   infoLst.foreach { info =>
      info match {
         case EmailAvailable(fName, _, email) =>

126

```
                    val data = (fName, email)
                    emailbuf += data
              case PhoneNoAvailable(fName, _,
phoneNo) =>

                       val data = (fName, phoneNo)
                       phonebuf += data
                 case OnlyName(fName, lName) =>
                       val data = (fName, lName)
                       namebuf += data
                 case c @ Contacted(_, _) =>
                       contactedbuf += c
        }
    }
```

//return the list accumulated in those buffers for further processing

(emailbuf.toList, phonebuf.toList, namebuf.toList, contactedbuf.toList)

}

Notice ignoring some members with underscore, and also the use of @ in the case of Contacted - as in this case the interest is the whole class instance rather than individual members.

...

This wraps up the case for the present discussion on pattern matching.

Covariance and Contravariance

"Progress of any kind is always at variance with the old and established ideas and therefore with the codes inspired by them."

Ludwig von Mises

The concept of Covariance and Contravariance are relevant to Object Oriented Paradigm, specifically the inheritance part of it. But it is not less so in case of Functional programming.

Functional programming is not opposed to object oriented programming. They are orthogonal concerns. Functions use objects (type of input and output – and that is where covariance and contrivance comes in really). [However one major point of difference(?) between FP and OOP perhaps - is in the mutual interaction of entities and functions. In OOP methods are called on objects directly, and that is a major communication path between objects. Whereas in FP major communication occurs through input and output, and calling methods on objects is somewhat incidental]

...

The prefix co- in english has a connotation of going with something (e.g. cooperation, coexistence). On the contrary, the prefix contra- has a connotation of going against something or someone.

Note that either of them implies two entities / bodies etc. (not just one). Because in order to cooperate with someone, there has two be two persons (or groups etc.) one who is cooperating, and one who is the recipient of the cooperation (i.e. with whom the cooperation is happening).

...

(Although not an exact definition) statistically 'variance' is a measure of variability [how far an individual data point is expected to vary from the central tendency.]

In software - extrapolating it loosely, covariance may be made sense of as the measure of something varying in the same way (or similar way) with something else. What are these two things that vary? They are two different structures. And on what axis this variation takes place. The axis is the class inheritance hierarchy.

More specifically when a structure varies in it's types in a similar fashion with the class inheritance hierarchy of another structure, they are covariant (or more specifically the second one is covariant to the first one). Contravariance is diametrically opposite to covariance. It implies the second structure varies in it's types in the reverse order of class hierarchy, compared to the first structure. It is like the opposite side of the same concept (a mirror reflection of sorts). And hence mastering the concept of covariance is enough to understand the concept of contravariance equally well.

Assignment compatibility vs variance

There is a scope that without proper familiarity, covariance may be confused with assignment compatibility.

Assignment compatibility
In object oriented programming, particularly in Java (and possibly in other languages too), you can assign a subclass to a variable of superclass type, without any issue.

Suppose you have an inheritance direction like -

Machine >: Car >: Sedan

I.e. Car is a subclass of machine and Sedan is a subclass of Car. [The inheritance hierarchy (from superclass to subclass) flows to the right.]

class Machine {}

class Car extends Machine {}

class Sedan extends Car {}

In this case, in Java, you can assign an instance of type *Sedan* to a variable of type *Car* (or an instance of either *Car* or *Sedan* to a variable of type *Machine*). i.e. instances of classes, which are lower in the hierarchy can be assigned to a variable of higher [super] types. The opposite is not true.

Car x = new Sedan(); //ok

Sedan y = new Car(); //not ok

In real world it makes sense. A sedan is a car, and a car is a machine. But not all machines are necessarily cars, or not all cars are necessarily sedan.

...

However this ability to assign an instance of a lower class to a variable of a higher class (in type inheritance hierarchy), does not imply covariance in any way. It is simply *assignment compatibility*. Assignment compatibility in this sense applies to a single line of hierarchy [without reference to a second line of hierarchy].

covariance

However, in order to have covariance (or contravariance for that matter), we need to have two different structures – each of them following one of two related lines of hierarchies. One of them is the recipient of covariance (like the recipient of cooperation), - *with which line of hierarchy, something is covariant* [In our example case - it is the line of hierarchy of these classes : Machine >: Car >: Sedan (left side denoting higher type in the hierarchy, and right side indicating more derived types)]

The other side, the other structural hierarchy, (i.e. the other structure following a similar line of hierarchy), which would be covariant to this one, would have come from a different structure, but should in some way be related to the first structural hierarchy. Such a relation occurs often in type constructors.

If you recall the earlier discussion (Chapter 3) about Type Constructors – *List* is an example of a *type constructor*. List has to be the List of something – i.e. a *List of Int* or a *List of String*. List takes another type (such as Int) to construct a concrete type (such as List[Int]). Hence List is a type constructor.

Let's take List as the other structure which we want to vary with the line of hierarchy of Machine >: Car >: Sedan. i.e. we are interested in exploring the *inheritance hierarchical relation between List[Machine], List[Car] and List[Sedan] on one hand and Machine, Car, Sedan on the other.*

If you see the definition of List class in Scala, you will find it shows *List[+A]* (+A means - type A or any of its covariant types). I.e. by definition List is a covariant type constructor (covariant to, or covariant in it's inner type – of which it is a List). Which means List of those three types (Machine, Car, Sedan) will be covariant with the hierarchical structure of those types themselves.

So covariance, for the covariant structure, implies - following along the same line of inheritance hierarchy as it's reference structure.

So given : (a) *Machine >: Car >: Sedan* and (b) *List to be covariant in it's inner type* we get : *List[Machine] >: List[Car] >: List[Sedan]*

I.e. List being covariant (in it's inner type) - List[Machine], List[Car], and List[Sedan] will follow the same hierarchical pattern as Machine, Car and Sedan themselves.

In summary :

A >: B >: C

plus Covariance (of List in this instance) =>

List[A] >: List[B] >: List[C]

...

In general if any type constructor is defined with a +T for an inner type (for example Stack[+T]), which means type T is to be used only in covariant positions for that type constructor – it implies that if B is a subtype of A, Stack[B] will be a subtype of Stack[A].

covariance in action : delivering machines
Now for a demonstration of covariance in action. Assume the same hierarchy -

Machine >: Car >: Sedan

Consider the following code -

```
class Machine {
        override def toString() = "of machines"
}


class Car extends Machine {
        override def toString() = "of cars"
}
```

```
class Sedan extends Car {
        override def toString() = "of sedans"
}
```

```
val machine: Machine = new Machine
val car: Car = new Car
val sedan: Sedan = new Sedan
```

```
def deliverMachine(machine: Machine): List[Machine] =
List(machine)
```

```
//ok
println("deliverMachine(machine) => " + deliverMachine(machine))
println("deliverMachine(car) => " + deliverMachine(car))
println("deliverMachine(sedan) => " + deliverMachine(sedan))
```

This code will produce -

deliverMachine(machine) => List(of machines)

deliverMachine(car) => List(of cars)

deliverMachine(sedan) => List(of sedans)

Note that *Machine* is the highest in hierarchy of the 3 classes. And hence a method which takes in a machine and delivers a List of Machines, has the freedom to deliver either a List of Machines, or a List of Cars, or a List of Sedans (This is possible because List is covariant).

However the choice will get restricted if you were to add

(to the same script) another method which delivers a List of Cars.

def deliverCar(car: Car): List[Car] = List(car)

println("deliverCar(car) => " + deliverCar(car))

println("deliverCar(sedan) => " + deliverCar(sedan))

This part should produce -

deliverCar(car) => List(of cars)

deliverCar(sedan) => List(of sedans)

Note that you cannot invoke this *deliverCar* method with a parameter of type *Machine*. If you try -

deliverCar(machine)

It would result in -

error: type mismatch;

found : this.Machine

required: this.Car

deliverCar(machine)

(The focus of error, pointing to the argument of call to deliverCar.)

This is more to do with assignment compatibility.

On the other hand, you can not have a method which takes a machine and delivers a List of Cars. Trying to define a method like -

def takeMachineDeliverCar(machine: Machine): List[Car] = List(machine)

Would result in -

error: type mismatch;

found   : this.Machine

required: this.Car

def takeMachineDeliverCar(machine: Machine): List[Car] =
List(machine)

(The focus of error, pointing to the input of the List constructor.)

So the function deliverMachine above, is the most general form of such functions, (which works because of covariance of Lists).

contravariance

It is simply a matter of logical extension to conclude that contravariance (applied to direction of inheritance hierarchy of two related structures) implies that the second structure has a inheritance hierarchical flow – which is opposite in direction to the flow of inheritance hierarchy of the first structure.

For a type constructor, where the inner type is to be used only in contravariant position (so the inner type would be denoted with a minus sign in front (for example Wallet[-T] – this is not an established type readily available in Scala – just for example) – the hierarchical relationship of constructed types would be such that, if B is a subtype of A, then Wallet[B] would be a super-type of Wallet[A].

Hence, given two types A and B such that -

A >: B

plus contravariance (of Wallet in it's inner type) =>

Wallet[A] <: Wallet[B]

contravariance in action : for a few more dollars

For an example of contravariance in action, assume the following hierarchy.

CoinOrNote >: DollarNote >: HighvalueDollarNote

Some coins(cents or dollars) or notes, which is subclassed into dollar notes, and then still further subclassed / extended into high value dollar notes.

class CoinOrNote

class DollarNote extends CoinOrNote

class HighvalueDollarNote extends DollarNote

Now let us think of different types of wallets with respect to these type of currencies. We have a class Wallet, which is contravariant in it's type parameter (*class Wallet[-T]*) - and we are interested in what type of coins or notes (of the three above classification) it can take.

class Wallet[-T]{

  def canTake(note: T): String = {

   if (note.isInstanceOf[HighvalueDollarNote]) "High value note"

   else if (note.isInstanceOf[DollarNote]) "Mid value note"

   else "May be a coin"

 }

}

Note that the method *canTake*, makes use of the type parameter, as it's argument type. (This is by design. More discussion will follow later in the chapter).

Now let us define some notes and some wallets of different types.

val coin: CoinOrNote = new CoinOrNote

val tenDollar: DollarNote = new DollarNote

val hundredDollar: HighvalueDollarNote = new HighvalueDollarNote

val pouch: Wallet[CoinOrNote] = new Wallet[CoinOrNote]

val noteWallet: Wallet[DollarNote] = new Wallet[DollarNote]

val executiveWallet: Wallet[HighvalueDollarNote] = new Wallet[HighvalueDollarNote]

Now about the real action. See what type of wallet can take what type of notes. The following calls work.

println(pouch.canTake(coin))

println(pouch.canTake(tenDollar))

println(noteWallet.canTake(tenDollar))

println(noteWallet.canTake(hundredDollar))

[Note that here the contravariance is applied in the method argument]. Pouch can take coin. On the other hand noteWallet can take dollar notes, high value or otherwise. However if you try -

println(noteWallet.canTake(coin))

That won't work. It produces an error message part of which would look like -

error: type mismatch;

found : this.CoinOrNote

required: this.DollarNote

println(noteWallet.canTake(coin))

(The focus of error - pointing at the input of the canTake method call)

So it can not go up in the hierarchy, and can take only *DollarNote* or more specialised class of that. ExecutiveWallet would eventually be more sophisticated(?) and will take only high value dollar notes.

Contrast this behaviour with that of the *acceptance of a List – about it's elements*. A *Sedan*, which is lowest in the hierarchy, could get into a *List of Machines* (*Machine* being the topmost in the hierarchy).

...

Hence (coming back to the dichotomy of variance and assignment compatibility,) *variance deals with the preservation of an assignment compatibility relationship across a transformation of types*. It is not about whether an instance of a subtype may be assigned to a variable of its super-type. Variance for inheritance hierarchy of a structure is - varying with, or varying against the inheritance hierarchy of another structure.

Invariant
In this context it is also possible to have an invariant relationship for class hierarchy. Which means there is no variance relationship between the class hierarchies of one set of types with another.

Note that unlike *List*, *Array* is an invariant type constructor. (Array[A]). (This was necessitated for type safety as - unlike List, Array is a mutable structure.)

Liskov substitution principle in context
There is a well known set of design principles for

designing classes and interfaces in Object oriented Design, named SOLID (the name is made by taking first letters of the names of 5 different principles). One of these principles (the L) is *Liskov Substitution Principle*. It goes like - "If for each object o1 of type S there is an object o2 of type T such that for all programs P defined in terms of T, the behaviour of P is unchanged when o1 is substituted for o2 then S is a subtype of T". In effect it specifies that - functions that use pointers of references to base classes must be able to use objects of derived classes without knowing it. Among other things it greatly helps reduced coupling between classes (which results in easier extension, without breaking the existing code).

This principle implies that the client dependencies of a class, should be amenable to be substituted by a subclass, without the client (of the class) having to know it (and hence needing to make any change). Drawing from our previous example – if somebody has asked for a Car, you can simply send a Sedan without any eyebrow being raised.

This requires a degree of behavioural conformance. If the client needs something (in the name of a Car) which he can drive from location A to location B, and which has leather sits, and ..., a Sedan also should have those features. Where a Sedan may differ, such as the shape of the boot, is not part of the basic behavioural signature of a car, but an enhancement which is of interest to you (but not to the client). The points of the basic behavioural signature (of a car), on which the car hire contract was signed, must be conformed to by the Sedan also. That way client is unaffected, and you can change your fleet of cars to any luxury models, in hope of better business in future, but buying the new models in such a way, that they at least tick all the boxes of the definition of a car (for the sake of existing contracts). Thus the specific functionality of the subclass may be different but it must conform to the expected behavioural signature of the base class.

In order to achieve this behavioural sub-typing, a set of protocols have to be maintained. The first (or rather the first two) of them being – (1) *parameters of the subclasses's methods should be contravariant to the matching parameters of those methods in the base class.* And (2) *return values of the subclasses's methods should be covariant to the return values of those methods in the base class.* [So contravariance in parameters and covariance in return values]. (And oh by definition a class is both contravariant and covariant to itself. Kind of like a greater than or equal to / less than or equal to relation.)

This means that the parameters in subclasses must either be the same types as those in the base class or must be less restrictive. And return types from subclass methods must be the same as, or more restrictive than, the return types of the equivalent base class methods. [As a rule contravariance is less restrictive and covariance is more restrictive.]

The Icon Rule

'Icon' is a mnemonic (I coined) for Input Contravariant. [remember I of I/O stands for input, and add 'con' for Contra to it]. As a rule, *contravariance is used for input positions* (or consumers) and *covariance for output positions* (or producers). [If type parameter has to be used as both output and input type, then it should be invariant.] (Note that the Icon rule is in keeping with the Liskov Substitution Principle)

There are exceptions to this such as - covariant type parameter can be used as method argument type, if lower bound is used. (i.e. guarded approach for exceptions).

...

A brief note on mutability :

Type parameter with variance annotation (covariant + or contravariant -) can be used as mutable field type, only if the field has object private scope (private[this]) in Scala.

Object private members can be accessed only from within the object in which they are defined. It turns out - that accesses to variables from the same object in which they are defined, do not cause problems with variance. It appears this is due to the fact that - references to such fields can not be exposed outside the containing object, and hence there is no question of replacing the reference with a statically weaker type.

Scala immutable container types such as Option and List are covariant in their type parameter.

...

In defence of variance
A strict type system protects the code against a lot of inadvertent mistakes, by catching some issues at compile time through type checking. However clever use of covariance and contravariance provide some flexibility to this checking within a framework (of compatible inheritance hierarchy). This allows for valid generalizations, (which would be impossible, in a purely invariant world).

To start with a somewhat intuitive explanation -

Firstly note that - (usually) the subclassing or extension goes from more general to more specific classes. So a superclass will (usually) be more generic than it's subclass. An animal would usually be extended to a Mammal, and that in turn would usually be extended to a Tiger for instance. (Deriving Mammal class from the Tiger class would require an unusual mind or an unusual purpose - I should think).

Some type of processing with any of those classes (in a

single line of hierarchy), may not need the specification beyond the top level. For instance if you are calculating age of an Animal, from it's date of birth, it would possibly be the same whether it is any type of Animal, or a Mammal, or specifically a Tiger. Hence keeping such a processing at the generic level of Animal, (but restricting it to that line of hierarchy - and not just applying it to anything which does not remotely have a concept of Date of Birth [and thus allowing for a good degree of type safety]), may just provide the right bit of flexibility, while still applying the rigour.

Coming back to our specific examples - It is likely that an executive wallet will be more sophisticated and expensive, so you wouldn't want to ruin it, by pushing a lot of heavy coins into it. But pouch may be more rugged and less costly. So can have more generic use. [However if you have a choice of taking - either a pouch with some coins in it, or an executive wallet with a lot of 100 dollar bills – I would say go for the executive wallet, and figure out later where you are going to keep your coins.] Hence where there is a need for generality at lesser cost, more flexibility can be provided by accepting Wallets of more general nature, but as the cost of wallet goes up, there may be need for more restrictive use, (of what goes in), so that the expensive wallet is not abused.

In case of Lists on the other hand – the same concept of generality works, but in terms of delivery (output). If you knew that – for machines in your scope of usage - you only have cars of certain sizes and within certain weight limit, or some similar or lesser sized and weighted machines, such as may be a motorbike, or a drivable trolley - you can carry all of those and deliver to the client using the same truck that you have at your disposal. Hence you can provide a method that outputs a more general type of covariant constructor (e.g. List[Machine]).

If on the other hand you knew your machines would

differ so widely in specification, that the same method of delivery would be inadequate for the case of one, or grossly above par for the case of the other (e.g. delivery of private cars, vs heavy artillery machines like military tanks), you need to have separate arrangement of delivery (multiple methods with more specific output types). Where there is some generality among the types - you can use midway, and have a method of delivery (e.g. from private cars downward, in terms of method output type it could be List[Car] - covariant structure but starting from a 'midway type in the hierarchy' as appropriate), - and can use another method of delivery for the more specialised cases.

Functional transformations

"You have to maintain a culture of transformation and stay true to your values"

Jeff Weiner

'Functional Transformation' is not a term in common use in context of functional programming. (It is more a mathematical concept indicating a function being 'transformed' through another function (the parallel is HOF). However I have picked up this term - which seemed (to me) appropriate, to describe - *transformation of data structures through series of functions* [Somewhat like a 'transformational pipeline']. This is a core aspect of FP, [although may not be known by this name]. The transformational pipeline, may contain one or more higher order functions.

For a quick glimpse of what I mean by a 'transformational pipeline', you may recall parts of the solution (code) from the very first chapter[given below] -

(1)

*def txnLst = for (line <-
Source.fromFile("tran.txt").getLines)*

yield(line.split(",") match { case Array(a,b,c,d) => (a.toInt, d.toDouble)})

(2)

if (!txnLst.map (_._1).toSet.contains(acct))

(3)

val balance = txnLst.flter(_._1 == acct).map(_._2).sum - amt

As you keep working in FP in earnest, you would possibly find the scope for plenty of such examples.

...

But before delving deeper into the subject, I intend to discuss the topic of data structures in brief. Because the transformations will need something to transform (that which will be transformed). And those are usually some type of data structures. (It is like - in order to drive you need a car).

A good understanding of data structures in general, and at least one data structure in particular, could go a long way to assimilate the concept of functional transformations applied to [or through] data structures.

What is data structure ?

The concept is elusively simple. A Data Structure is *any structure that holds data*. As simple as that. Although as I mentioned, it is elusively simple. Because it is rather difficult to be satisfied with such a definition without any explanation.

Two words are important here. *Data* and *Structure*. Note that what we implicitly mean by data is not just a number, or a String, (or even a set of numbers for that matter). What makes those "data", is the context. For instance if I were to tell you 177, it may not convey much to you. But If I were to tell you that my height is 177cm, then that is contextual, and that becomes data.

In the same way, 'Arnie', 'Sutherland', 'Lida' 162, 181 etc. may not be data - unless you put them in a context - like say first name, last name and height (in cm) of employees in a company [which may be used for the purpose of some analysis, for instance]

Arnie SutherLand 181

Lida Zaniska 162

Corbyn Arnold 179

...

And a data structure is a 'structure' that holds data. Why structure is necessary to hold data? The intuitive answer - for similar reason anything else is put into a well defined structure - for better and/or easier - storage, retrieval, manipulation, transportation and so on. Eventually data structures (especially the prominent ones which are collective in nature) are different from each other by their memory usage and performance characteristics. Each of them is geared towards serving certain purpose(s) well, and are to be chosen based on the use case. But before getting into this kind of structures, a little discussion in generality.

Algebraic Data Types

A data structure can be any structure that holds data, the are usually collective in nature - although (1) at any point the collection may have zero, one or more elements (2) Each member in the collection may not have the same structure (although where they differ - the possible types have to be from a defined finite set.)

In computer programming, especially in functional programming - an algebraic data type is a kind of composite type - a type formed by combining other types. [ADT is very relevant to data structures]

Two common classes of algebraic types are product types (i.e., tuples and records) and sum types, also called tagged or disjoint unions or variant types.

...

Each value (or each data member) of a 'product type' - typically consists of several values, called fields. All values of that type have the same combination of field types. [Hence a single value is practically a record in the collection].

For example consider records of all students in a school. Each record may contain, name, date of birth, class and so on, but each record would very likely have the same structure. So those records collectively, would be an instance of product type.

...

In 'sum type' on the other hand any individual value (data member), could be one of several (but [usually] few predefined variety) structural category, called variants.

A value of a variant type is usually created with a quasi-functional entity called a constructor. Each variant has its own constructor, which takes a specified number of arguments with specified types. The set of all possible values of a sum type is the set-theoretic sum, i.e., the disjoint union, of the sets of all possible values of its variants. (Enumerated types are a special case of sum types in which the constructors take no arguments, as exactly one value is defined for each constructor.)

...

For example consider a Student record being constructed (with a constructor) like -

class Student(fName: String, lName: String, dob: Date, year: Int)

And that of a teacher being constructed as -

class Teacher(fName: String, lName: String, position:String, major:String)

Now consider planning of teaching for a particular year for say year 10, section H. It will possibly consist of a fixed number of known students and fixed number of teachers to teach various subjects in rotation through periods [period pattern repeating usually every week]. So a data structure, for

147

personnel in the teaching plan, would possibly consist of two types - the students and the teachers. And each individual personnel picked from the collection, would be either a student variety or a teacher variety. [The type of any single person in such a collection - would be either a student variant or a teacher variant, and all possible values of a persons type is set-theoretic sum of student type and teacher type]

...

Values of algebraic types are analysed with pattern matching, which identifies a value by its constructor or field names and extracts the data it contains.

A data structure, which is collective in nature (i.e. a collection of lot of individual records), may follow one of the two types (sum or product), or may even combine the two, for example - each record themselves may be a sum (or disjoint union) type.

...

Coming back to the data structure question - each data (each single data, data member) in a data structure, is an individual data point [that may also be associated with a numeric or associative index or pointer - for easy/unambiguous identification of location etc.]

Suppose you are analysing data for housing. You may have collected thousands (millions?) of individual house/apartment buy-sell records with details for each case - such as suburb, postcode, number of bedrooms, number of toilets, which floor each is situated, floor area, ..., price of sale, date and so on. You intend to analyse them - slicing and dicing it on various cross sections, e.g. a trend for house pricing (of similar size) over a period of few years, or in the same year but from centre of city to outer suburbs, or .... Each of the house record is a single data point (data member) in your data structure.

Note that [one point about the basic importance of data structures (or data collections)] these data individually will have no (or not much) informational value. You have sold your house, of such and such description, on such and such date, at such and such price, will become irrelevant as time goes by. Unless you know the pattern of house price rise across the same type of houses in similar type of locations, it may not help your friend decide how much he should pay for a house he is planning to buy. However taking all the data collectively, and analysing it intelligently - answers to a lot of questions may be found (at least within a statistical ballpark) even as a matter of predictive projections. That is where the collectivity of data gains in importance.

...

A Data Structure is any structure that holds data. However each variety of data structures - has their own relative arrangement of data [with or without explicit, numeric or associative index]. A List stores it's data members relative to each other in a certain arrangement. A Map does in it's own relative arrangement, which is different from that of List. (If it were the same, it would have been the same data structure.). And as mentioned before – different data structures have different memory usage and performance characteristics. This characteristics depend upon the relative arrangement and implicit / explicit indexing of the data members in the structure. [In other words how you store makes it what it is, and perform the way it does.]

data structures vs collections

In some context data structures and collections are considered a dichotomy. However in a broader scope [in my view], they are really same in essence. If anything, a data structure in it's purity, may be considered an abstraction of the *design of 'relative arrangement and indexing' of the data storage*, whereas a collection may be an implementation of the structure. Thus Array is a data structure and Array (API) in Scala or Java is an implementation of that abstraction, (and in still another aspect, in FP and Array is a type constructor, because it takes another type to construct a complete data type - e.g. Array[String]).

A data structure may be further refined in it's design to achieve gain in memory foot print and/or performance characteristics. Such as Map to HashTable and Tree to Balanced Binary Tree

Importance of collective data
I have already mentioned the aspect of predictive possibility for collective data. But I would like to mention a few other points regarding the usefulness of well structured data collections. [Although I am pretty sure, the usefulness does not stop only at the cases mentioned here.]

- A well structured data collection may serve as a historical reference of information.

- In some cases a set of data has meaning only collectively. For instance if you wish to know the current balance of an account, you can not do it with only a single transaction. You will have to know a reference balance in the past (it could be the opening balance or something more recent), and all transactions on the account thereafter. [So a single transaction record in isolation is meaningless for the balance calculation.]

- Talking about transaction, a financial transaction is often a two way street. somebody pays the money and somebody takes it (for instance in exchange of some goods or services). If you caught only one leg of the transaction (e.g. deduction from account A) and not the other leg (e.g. credit to account B), this would create account nightmare of sorts, (among other things). A single leg of transaction, in isolation, is a bad idea. Hence so much rigour on transactional integrity in software development.

- Processing of data may be more efficient when done on collectivity, rather than chasing after individual data here and there (for a similar reason, that mass production is cheaper). You can put special arrangements in place to enhance a particular type of processing, and it would be more cost-effective on collective data. [When a bank for instance - spends a few million dollars to automate a part of it's processing - it would usually do so for all the clients requiring such processing, and not leave behind some client record to be processed manually - unless there, the processing requires some special handling (i.e. it is not the same processing)]

List - a functional data structure

Let us get into the discussion of a specific data structure now. *List*. Many of our functional transformation examples will be based on List (although I intend to discuss a few other structures in brief - to illustrate some functional transformation examples better).

What is List
Chance is that you are already familiar with the data structure *List*. (As far as data structures are concerned, it's description should lie in the relative arrangement of it's data members [elements], along with indexing detail). In it's most general form, (which is LinkedList or singly linked list), a List is a collection of elements where each unit (except for the terminal one) consists of a data member and a pointer to the next element. [For the terminal element there is no data member, (and there is obviously no next element). Hence this has a

different type than the other units of a list]. In Scala list is immutable.

Hence List has two constructors (one representing the terminal element, and one for creating a List by adding a data member in front of an existing List. Note that in Scala, the pointer to the next element is abstracted away from the user of a List [managed internally]). In Scala the terminal element is represented as an object Nil (it corresponds to an empty list [and an empty list, in general, could be an empty list of any type. Because - if it does not have a data member, the type of it's data member does not matter]).

So we have a Nil constructor which is a case object, and a Cons (expressed as :: in Scala) constructor which is of the form *::(head, tail)* or may even be represented as *head :: tail* [because cons(i.e. ::) is also a method on List - and being a method ending in ':' it is a method on the right operand (which is *tail* in this case) is a List]

Note that Nil is a list in itself (an empty List). But Cons constructor needs *an element and a List* to start with. That *List* for Cons could be *Nil*. So you can add the first element (other than *Nil* - say an element *x*) in the List as x :: Nil [There are other syntaxes possible to achieve the same thing, such as List(x)]

Why List

Singly linked list (the List in Scala), is possibly the most ubiquitous of functional data structures. (And by definition all functional data structures are immutable). Why is it so? Some argument in it's favour being -

(1) Lists are possibly the simplest sort of data structure that can be created in a functional language, purely at the language level (as opposed to - for instance arrays, which end up exposing a few extra details about the underlying machine [i.e. contiguous memory].) List can be defined as nested pairs, or

lambdas (based on the language, but in any reasonably advanced FP language it should be possible).

(2) List, being a recursive data type, are naturally amenable to the normal functional style using recursion instead of iteration. At each step, you process the first element and recurse on the rest. This works because the rest of the list is a list itself (in fact, this is exactly what 'recursive data type' means). A recursive function on list - like this, naturally follows the "shape" of the data structure.

List being a sum type data structure, at each step of recursion, the List may have one of two possible shapes. It may match either be a Nil or a Cons constructor. These can be handled as two separate cases. The Cons case handles both the first field (the topmost element - whatever needs to be done with it [the laterality]) - and the second field (the rest of the list) is usually passed on to the next level of recursion [the stepping]). The Nil case signals the end of the list [the stopping] and should be reserved for wrap up activities and return of final result as applicable.

(Arrays, on the other hand, do not naturally lend themselves to recursion. There's no natural way to split an array into the current element and the rest of the array. Instead, you're expected to keep track of an index explicitly, which makes recursive code uglier and opens you up to potential problems like off-by-one errors.)

(3) Immutable lists are naturally a persistent data structure. The elements themselves are stored, and in references to Lists, the pointers get shared. So when for a value *lst1* which hold a List like *Cons of x and xs* [i.e *lst1* = ::(x, xs)], *lst1* actually has the pointer to the top of the list *x :: xs*, and when *xs* is passed to another value, that would have the pointer to the top element of *xs* (which stands independently as a list from the

original list *lst1*, but in effect is sharing all the elements in place except the first one of the original list). This avoids having to copy the whole list here and there, while still preserving immutability. (Arrays, on the other hand, cannot reuse memory like this.)

Construction of List

List is a sealed abstract class in Scala -

sealed abstract class List[+A] extends Seq[A]

with two known subclasses -

Nil and *::* (known as Cons)

The common way of creating a List (of say Ints) would be something like

val intLst = List(1, 2, 3)

[Actually the arguments in this case are passed to the apply method of the List Object which has signature -

def apply [A](xs : A) : List[A]*

and it creates a list with given elements, taking variable number of (same type) arguments]

Normally (usual convention) the apply method of an object returns a new instance of the Class with the same name as an object. However the List class being a sealed abstract class - can not be instantiated.

In this particular case the List Object returns a new instance of the Cons subclass.

the rsult of the above apply method can be represented in nested form like -

val intLst = 1 :: (2 :: (3 :: Nil))

(note that a method that ends in a ':' is a method on the

operand to its right)

So the Cons(::) method on the Nil object takes the 3 as a parameter and produces an anonymous instantiation of the Cons class with 3 as its head and a reference to the Nil object as its tail. Lets call this anonymous object c1. The Cons method is then called on c1 taking 2 as its parameter returning a new anonymous Cons instantiation lets call it c2, which has 2 for its head and a reference to c1 as its tail. Then finally the cons method on the c2 object takes the 1 as a parameter and returns the named object with 1 as its head and a reference to c2 as its tail.

Or in a more plane form it goes like -

val intLst = 1 :: 2 :: 3 :: Nil

...

Construction of an empty List (of say Ints), can be done as -

scala> val x = List[Int]()

x: List[Int] = List()

or

scala> val y = Nil

y: scala.collection.immutable.Nil.type = List()

However, note that in the second case the inner is yet not known. However, once an element of certain type is added in front of the empty List, the correct type is inferred.

scala> val lst1 = ::(1, y)

lst1: scala.collection.immutable.::[Int] = List(1)

Perhaps in normal coding practice it is good to stick to List[Int]() and List(1,2,3) type of form, for such creations.

...

In a very similar way, you can create an empty List for String with List[String]() and a List (of Strings) with given elements like List("abc", "def")

...

When you provide values that are less specific (e.g. one Int and one String), the common type is inferred.

scala> val lst1 = List(1, "abc")

<console>:11: warning: a type was inferred to be `Any`; this may indicate a programming error.

   val lst1 = List(1, "abc")

        ^

lst1: List[Any] = List(1, abc)

If you wish to avoid that (may be by mistake you inserted 1, you wanted to have List of "1", and "abc"), spell the type, and the check will be more rigourous.

scala> val lst2 = List[String](1, "abc")

<console>:11: error: type mismatch;

found   : Int(1)

required: String

   val lst2 = List[String](1, "abc")

        ^

Perhaps time to get into our discussion proper. Which is *functional transformations.*

Transformations on List

In this section, transformations on Lists will be mainly

discussed. However many of the transformations discussed here (perhaps all) are available in other prominent data structures (such as *Map*) and they mean similar transformation (but as applicable to that structure).

map

The term *mapping* in functional programming (and hence the map function) relates to the concept of transforming the values from one domain to another. Or *mapping a point of one domain into the corresponding point in another domain.*

For instance if you have a domain of the radii of a lot of circles, and another domain with areas of those circles, the mapping of one point of the first domain to the corresponding point of the second domain, would be through something like - area(r) = PI * r * r. And the function, which is conceptually the arrow of transformation (from a point of the first domain, to the corresponding point in the second domain) is known as the mapping function (in this case area(r) = PI * r * r).

The 'map' transformation (or 'map' function) in a way facilitates this mapping to happen between the domains, using the mapping function.

...

Note that the function 'map' is not the mapping function itself, but it is an HOF which takes the mapping function as argument. In a manner of speaking it lifts the mapping function (which would be applicable to an individual element or data point) to be applicable to the entire structure holding such data points (and representing the domain to be transformed).

Also notable is that the mapping function has to be an unary function, whose argument should be of type which is the type of the individual elements of the data structure, on which the map is applied. And it produces a data structure whose structure type (but not necessarily the type of containing element) is the same as that of the input structure, and whose size also is same as the size of the input structure. The mapping function could be either a regular function or an anonymous function / lambda.

What is the point of having such a function?

Firstly, note that the mapping function is a function which is defined on a single data point, not the whole structure (in this case radius r). But 'map' gives a way to transform the elements of the structure (under the hood, in a manner of speaking), using the mapping function, and gives you a similar data structure with the transformed objects (which may be, and quiet often are, of a different type). So if you have a function, that works on a single object, and the 'map' function, you can use it to transform the whole structure (in a processing pipeline), without separately bringing the objects, out of the structure by yourself. [Sort of - map this domain to that domain, using this transformation function].

Looking at it from another perspective - you could say that - it can be used to lift a function that works on only one value to an equivalent function that works on an entire collection. And this lifting of the function helps in 'transformational pipelining' so that beginning of one processing can be plugged seamlessly at the end of another processing, both working on List. (a suitable example soon follows)

For example - length is a function on String which provides it's length (size of characters). So it takes a String and returns an Int. (String) => Int

scala> "abc".length

reso: Int = 3

Now if we take a List of Strings and map it through the

length function, what happens?

scala> val lst1 = List("I", "am", "going", "home")

lst1: List[String] = List(I, am, going, home)

scala> lst1.map(_.length)

res2: List[Int] = List(1, 2, 5, 4)

It provides a List (of the same size as the original list) where each element is the result of applying the function used within map [the inner function] on each of the elements in the original list (in that order). Note that in the map you need the function applied, or called on the argument [which with placeholder syntax becomes -.length] rather than just the function name. The argument is each element of the original list in turn (map is designed to apply each element of the List in turn.)

...

Instead of placeholder syntax, this could have been applied through a lambda (with named argument) also.

scala> lst1.map(str => str.length)

res3: List[Int] = List(1, 2, 5, 4)

...

'map' is a somewhat universal transformation, and applies to possibly all basic data structures in Scala, including Map (the structure) and Option. However it's field of applicability may be different based on the actual structure it is applied to. For instance for a List the input type of the inner function has to be the element type of the List. However for a Map (structure) it needs to be a (key, value) pair.

...

Previously, in context of 'transformational pipelining' I mentioned about - 'beginning of one processing can be plugged seamlessly at the end of another processing, both working on List'. Let's see what it is about.

If you wanted the total length of the strings taken together from the above list of strings (lst1) you could do -

scala> lst1.map(_.length).sum

reso: Int = 12

There is a function *sum* defined for list of Numeric values. Since map on a List yields another List in output, (and in this case the output List is Numeric), it is possible to call sum directly on the output. In this case sum could be plugged in at the end of map processing, because map has an output type which is List, and sum takes an input type List (although restricted to Numeric type lists). When your familiarity grows with different types of transformations, you may feel more comfortable, joining those other type of transformations, (along with map as required), to create longer chains of transformational pipelining.

So one (and perhaps the main) utility of map is to lift a function for '(transformational) pipeline compliance'. But wise use of such generic HOF may lead to other benefits.

If for instance you wanted to count the elements in the List, you could easily define your own count method using map and sum as follows -

scala> def count[A](lst: List[A]): Int = lst.map(_ => 1).sum

count: [A](lst: List[A])Int

scala> count(lst1)

res8: Int = 4

(Note that the same result could have been achieved by calling size on the list in this case, but the above is for illustration, and presents an idea for innovative use of map function [which is not just restricted to defining count])

Here the inner function is mapping each element (irrespective of what it is - to 1) (Note the underscore in the inner function. You don't particularly care what the string [individual element] is - so it is underscore). In a way, that is how things are counted. You take a 1 for each of the items and sum them.

filter

This is our next transformational function, which works on many data structures (and perhaps almost as ubiquitous as map). What does it do? well *it filters* (based on a criteria). The criteria being an inner function - which takes the type of a single element of the data structure (say a List) and return a Boolean). So for a List[A] the criteria (or predicate as it is sometimes called) would be a function of type A => Boolean.

filter function (an HOF) will take this function and return the elements for which the predicate is true, in a similar data structure (e.g. a List). Unlike map though, filter is not guaranteed to return the same number of elements as the input List, rather it is very likely to be a reduced List (and may even be an empty List - if for each of the elements the predicate returns false).

Note that this is also in a way, a lifting function, that takes a function - the predicate, which can make a decision on a single element - and raises the function as a criteria to be applied to the whole structure (and thus helping the plug-in of transformational pipelining, as discussed earlier).

For instance in the above list of Strings [List("I", "am", "going", "home")], if you were to get only the words with length > 3, you could do the following -

scala> lst1.filter(_.length > 3)

reso: List[String] = List(going, home)

Or if you want to get a list of words that does not contain the letter 'o' (lowercase) you could do -

scala> lst1.filter(!_.contains("o"))

res2: List[String] = List(I, am)

Any criteria that you can reasonably apply to elements of the list, you can filter the list with.

...

Eventually filter and map can be joined in a pipeline.

scala> lst1.filter(_.length > 3).map(_.length).sum

res4: Int = 9

But since filter (potentially) reduces a list, it is advisable in general, to push it earlier in the processing, which can reduce possible processing down the line (number of elements to be processed downstream reduces).

One example (although not very practical) illustrates this point -

the following map replaces 'o' with 'a'

scala> lst1.map(_.replaceAll("o","a"))

res3: List[String] = List(I, am, gaing, hame)

And suppose we want to get the uppercase equivalent of words with length greater than 3 in the final list. We could do this obviously -

scala> lst1.map(_.replaceAll("o","a")).filter(_.length > 3).map(_.toUpperCase)

res7: List[String] = List(GAING, HAME)

In this case the function replaceAll had to work on 4 arguments. But with a slight rearrangement (as shown below) the replacement can work on an already reduced list.

scala> lst1.filter(_.length > 3).map(_.replaceAll("o","a")).map(_.toUpperCase)

res8: List[String] = List(GAING, HAME)

And the final result is unaltered.

Anatomy of map and filter

How can you define a transformational function like map ?

It is an interesting exercise for an aspiring functional programmer, as it provides insight into how the inner function of the HOF (the HOF in this case being *map*) applies to each element, as well as how the recursion occurs through the structure. It also provides greater familiarity with the function itself.

Firstly, note that map works on some type A (which is the inner type of a List in this case), and needs a function (the mapping function) which takes in values of this type (A), and outputs a value of another type say type (B) [That is the most general form. In specific cases type B may be same as type A. For instance you take an Int and all the mapping function does is multiply it by 2, thereby yielding another Int]

So it needs a List[A] to convert, and a function A => B to convert the elements of the List with. So if you are to write a similar function - it will be polymorphic in types A and B. The signature (non-infix syntax) could be -

def myMap[A,B](lst: List[A], fn: A => B): List[B]

[Note that since this function is not defined in the class *List,* (and we are not planning to use the implicit conversion trick to make it infix), we will go the non-infix way - taking the list to be converted also as an explicit input]

The following will work -

```
def myMap[A,B](lst: List[A], fn: A => B): List[B] = lst match {
  case h :: t => fn(h) :: myMap(t, fn)
  case Nil => Nil
}
```

And this is how you can test it (add this after the function in the script) -

```
val lst = List("I", "am", "going", "home")
val myFunc: String => Int = str => str.length
val lengthLst = myMap(lst, myFunc)
println(lengthLst)
```

which should yield -

```
List(1, 2, 5, 4)
```

Since this is polymorphic in A and B, type of the input function needed explicit definition (String => Int), so that *map* can identify what type A and B will be. a lambda like _.length will not work here.

The things to note about the function is - (1) it matches on two possible cases (2) for non-empty case, it applies the head element to the inner function (as it should) and recurses on the *tail*. *tail* recursion will continue until it reaches the final *tail* which is Nil.

On the very first iteration applied to a List as shown above - the *h::t* form would actually be like -

```
"I" :: List("am", "going", "home")
```

Hence [not putting in the converted result of fn, but keeping it in call form] the expansion would unravel like -

fn("I") :: myMap(List("am", "going", "home")) then

fn("I") :: fn("am") :: myMap(List(going", "home")) then

fn("I") :: fn("am") :: fn("going") :: myMap(List("home")) then

fn("I") :: fn("am") :: fn("going") :: fn("home") :: Nil

Nil is the stopping condition and recursion will stop. At this stage (after conversion of individual values through fn, at appropriate points) the List may be returned (and that would be of type List[B], in this case List[Int])

...

Note that this definition is not tail recursive. In order to define it in a tail recursive way, you would need an inner function. The following works -

```scala
def myMap[A,B](lst: List[A], fn: A => B): List[B] = {
  import scala.collection.mutable.ListBuffer


  val acc = ListBuffer[B]()
  @annotation.tailrec
  def go(lst: List[A], fn: A => B, acc:ListBuffer[B]): List[B] = lst match {
    case h :: t => go(t, fn, acc += fn(h))
    case Nil => acc.toList
  }


  go(lst, fn, acc)
```

}

Here the accumulated list of output at each stage, is also passed as an argument to the inner function.

...

The definition of filter is not too far off. The following -

```scala
def myFilter[A](lst: List[A], fn: A => Boolean): List[A] = {
import scala.collection.mutable.ListBuffer

val acc = ListBuffer[A]()
@annotation.tailrec
def go(lst: List[A], fn: A => Boolean, acc:ListBuffer[A]): List[A] =
lst match {
  case h :: t => go(t, fn, if (fn(h)) acc += h else acc)
  case Nil => acc.toList
}

go(lst, fn, acc)
}

val lst = List("I", "am", "going", "home")
val myFunc: String => Boolean = str => str.length > 3
val lengthLst = myFilter(lst, myFunc)
println(lengthLst)
```

should yield -

```scala
List(going, home)
```

Except for the fact the myFilter is polymorphic in only one type (the output of the inner function is always Boolean in case of filter), the crux of difference lies in how the recursion step is handled.

contrast -

case h :: t => go(t, fn, if (fn(h)) acc += h else acc)

with that of the myMap case -

case h :: t => go(t, fn, acc += fn(h))

Here instead of straightaway adding the head element applied to inner function [fn(h)] it checks the output of the inner function applied to the element. If it passes (true), it adds the element itself (not the output of function application) to the accumulated list, otherwise it passes the accumulated list, as it is, to the next recursion step.

Time to move on to our next transformation, which is *fold*.

fold

'map' was about mapping from one domain to another, and 'filter' was about filtering (out) some elements. What does fold do. Well it folds. But for a List, what does that mean?

Think of a long advertisement pamphlet with multiple folds, and a glossy outer cover (kind of a holder of the pamphlet). When it is open, it may be rather long. but when you collapse (fold) it, based on the shape of the folds - one part may get on top of another, then the third part on top of the already folded accumulation of first two parts and so on. Here, folding one part onto another is bringing the two parts together.

If you generalize the meaning of 'bringing together' as 'combining', then you got the meaning of fold as applicable to a data structures (e.g. List).

Given a way of combining one part with thus far accumulated whole (represented by a different type) [Think of it as a compact piece. In case of the pamphlet it could be the glossy holder, along with thus far folded part of the pamphlet]), *a collection can be reduced to a single compact element* (of that different type - which obviously is the output type).

Fold takes this way of combining (of one element with an accumulated whole type) in the form of an inner function and wraps up (or folds - in a manner of speaking), the elements of the collection one by one, into this compact accumulated whole - using this given 'way of combining', and finally delivers the compacted output.

...

In a sense, functional transformations (at least some of the conspicuous ones), can be categorized by wider generality of their function, and it may help understand them better. For instance, you could think of -

'map' as 'transformational' - in the sense that it transforms each individual element (without making any distinctive selection)

'filter' is 'selective' - in the sense that it selects elements based on a criteria (but does not transform) and

'foldLeft' or 'foldRight' (generically fold) as 'aggregating' - in the sense it attempts to combine the elements into a single whole.

[If you are to now guess which of these 3 categories would be more suited to implement a function like 'sum' - what would your guess be?]

There are other functions which may belong to one of these categories. For instance *dropWhile* (not introduced yet) is selective in nature and *reduce* (not introduced yet) is aggregating in nature. And there are other categories such as 'grouping' or 'dividing into groups' (of which *groupBy* could be one possible member) and 'pairing' (of which *zip* would be a candidate).

...

Note that for a linear structure (like a multifold pamphlet) you may choose to fold it starting from the left hand side, or the right hand side. For a List, *fold* comes in two flavours - *foldLeft* and *foldRight*. (Start folding from the left side or the right side.).

The signatures are as follows -

def foldLeft[B](z: B)(op: (B, A) => B): B

def foldRight[B](z: B)(op: (A, B) => B): B

B is the final return type, as well as the type of the initial value z. It is the compacted type. Think if you were putting single sheets of paper on a stack of papers, and you consider a single sheet as a different type from a stack, then A would be of type single sheet of papers, and B would be the stack of paper type, which will also be the type of the final outcome (which would be a stack of papers).

The function 'op' which combines the individual element [type A] with the compacted accumulation [type B] takes the argument in different order in foldRight compared to foldLeft. In foldRight, the compacted type comes at the right (second) argument.

Think of foldLeft (and the logic may be applied in similar fashion to foldRight). Say you have the list which you want to consume from left to right. So you put the initial value of the compacted element type (say an empty holder) on the left of the whole list, and you pick out elements, one by one, from the left side of the list. So for a List like -

1 :: 2 :: 3 :: 4 :: Nil

the arrangement would be like -

[initial compact value] [1 :: 2 :: 3 :: 4 :: Nil]

or more concretely as -

[z] [1 :: 2 :: 3 :: 4 :: Nil]

And the first thing you try - is to combine the initial compact value (z) with leftmost element of List (1 in this case). So you are taking the elements of the List, in that order, in the function (for foldLeft)

op(z, 1) or op of ([type B], [type A])

Now since the output type of op is B (the compacted type), naturally when you are ready to combine the second element with the already compacted accumulation you still end up with type B on the left and type A on the right for the op. So it goes like this -

foldLeft of ([z] [1 :: 2 :: 3 :: 4 :: Nil])

op([z of type B], [1 of type A]) repeat with [2 :: 3 :: 4 :: Nil]

op([op(z,1) of type B] [2 of type A]) repeat with [3 :: 4 :: Nil]

op([combined value of type B] [3 of type A]) repeat with [4 :: Nil]

...

You get the general idea. The order of types in the input argument of op [which is B, A for foldLeft], is maintained through the folding process automatically.

fold and tail recursion
A List may be long, and making a process like flow not tail recursive would be risking stack overflow.

However, note that a List is a structure, which by definition is open on the left end.

1 :: 2 :: 3 :: 4 :: Nil

Nil is the bottommost entity, and elements in a List are consumed naturally from top [or left - if you prefer to call it that] (h :: t). If you need the next element, it is natural to take the head (h), which occurs on the left. The tail (t) is the rest [and itself a List]

What that means in terms of left vs right fold is that - foldLeft can be naturally implemented in a tail-recursive manner, and foldRight can not [There is an indirect way whereby you can implement foldRight using foldLeft and that would be tail recursive implementation. But it obviously can not be termed as 'natural'].

...

In my view, a somewhat intuitive understanding of why it is so, is that - folding operation, at each stage requires a single element from the List (which is the type A argument for the op). But since List is open at the left, it is natural to get the leftmost element first (and thus begin consuming from left end). [See the way it is consumed from left as explained above.] However for the rightmost element to be available first the whole list has to unravel from left to right, (and the elements stacked somehow), and then once the rightmost element is consumed, it will have to be traversed in the opposite direction through the stacked value.

...

Considering the natural tail-recursive nature of foldLeft, for this section (and rest of the chapter), I will be taking examples of foldLeft (unless there is a specific requirement for a topic, to show foldRight example).

foldLeft examples

Given the following list of Ints -

```
scala> val lsti = List(3,0,6,8)
lsti: List[Int] = List(3, 0, 6, 8)
```

sum can be easily found using foldLeft as follows -

```
scala> val sumi = lsti.foldLeft(0)(_ + _)
sumi: Int = 17
```

Note that the operation (op) here is using a lambda with placeholder syntax. The op (here) simply means, the single element for each fold (operation) is just added to the accumulated value.

...

You can calculate factorial 5 using foldLeft -

```
scala> val lsti2 = (1 to 5).toList
lsti2: List[Int] = List(1, 2, 3, 4, 5)


scala> val fact5 = lsti2.foldLeft(1)(_ * _)
fact5: Int = 120
```

In fact you can implement a factorial function in single line for positive integers (ignoring the zero / negative integers)

```
scala> def facto(n: Int) = (1 to n).toList.foldLeft(1)(_ * _)
facto: (n: Int)Int


scala> facto(4)
reso: Int = 24
```

...

Fold can be used in conjunction with map or any other suitable function transformations in a pipeline, so long as the input / output type for the plug-in is compatible.

Raising and lowering to the level

So far the transformations discussed in detail, has one common characteristic. They all take a List to work on. But what happens when you are given a lower order type than a List - like a single element, or a higher order type than a List like a List of Lists.

The physical process of ramming or rolling an uneven ground into a level, may be called flattening. If we generalise the meaning slightly - to say raising or lowering something to the same flat level (the same plane as it were), then we can include both lowering something from List of Lists to List as making it flat, and raising something from a single element to a List (not necessarily a List of the same type of elements) also as making it flat. This has bearing on the next two transformations discussed. Either of these may come handy, when used appropriately, in making a higher or lower order structure pluggable to a transformation pipeline, by changing it into a compliant structure.

flatten

Scala List has a flatten method, which reduces a List of Lists to a List (but containing all elements from the original List of Lists).

scala> val lstlst = List(List(1, 2), List(2,3), List(2,4,5))

lstlst: List[List[Int]] = List(List(1, 2), List(2, 3), List(2, 4, 5))

scala> lstlst.flatten

reso: List[Int] = List(1, 2, 2, 3, 2, 4, 5)

Note that the order is preserved.

...

As you can imagine, if you are given a List of Lists (of say Int) and you needed to calculate the sum of all the elements, you just need to flatten it first, before calling the sum on the flattened List.

flatMap

'flatMap' is an ubiquitous functional transformation, and along with map, has a very special place in functional transformations. [A great many functional structures and composite transformations, depend on map and flatMap].

As the name suggests, 'flatMap' has both the element of 'map' and 'flatten'. It *maps* in the sense that - it maps each element of a List (for flatMap on List) , through a function. But the mapping function here produces a List type (unlike 'map' where the mapping function is of general type A => B, for flatMap the mapping function is generally of the form A => List[B]). So eventually each mapped element from the original List creates a List (of element type B), of it's own. So the final deliverable (which would otherwise be of type List[List[B]]) needs to be 'flattened' to bring and down a level and finally deliver List[B]. In this sense flatMap flattens.

Here is the signature -

final def flatMap[B](f: (A) => GenTraversableOnce[B]): List[B]

(This technically is not same as A => List[B] [as mentioned by me earlier] but a more general form. But I mentioned that *the mapping function is generally of the form A => List[B]*. For the purpose of our discussion I would stick to the form A => List[B]. As that would be more generalised, and better for understanding purposes. *Besides GenTraversableOnce is a trait of which List is a subclass,* So even though the signature, that I put forth, differs from the recent official version, it is not too far off. The principle of flatMapping remains. Note the discussion that follows.)

Note that at some point (some earlier version) the signature could have been expressed as (non-infix form)

def flatMap[A,B](as: List[A])(f: A => List[B]): List[B]

and The inner function (f) is now more generalised. However GenTraversableOnce is a trait of which List is a subclass (among many others). Hence a function f: A => List[B] will be perfectly acceptable even in this shape (i.e. such a function could be readily passed to the current version of flatMap for Lists, without any modification). [And for our purpose let's use it *as if* it had the signature -

def flatMap[B](f: (A) => List[B]): List[B]

that will simplify understanding of the discussion.]

...

For a very simple example, note that *toList* function an a String, 'listifies' (converts into a list of) it's containing characters.

scala> "abcd".toList

res1: List[Char] = List(a, b, c, d)

So we have a function that takes a A String and returns a List of Chars. *String => List[Char]*

Now if we have a *List of Strings*, we can flatMap it with this function as inner function.

scala> List("I","am","going","home").flatMap(_.toList)

res2: List[Char] = List(I, a, m, g, o, i, n, g, h, o, m, e)

Following the types

In the journey of functional transformations, and sometimes implementing one HOF in terms of other functions - it is quite useful to try to follow the types. I.e. looking at what is the type of the function you are trying to build up (in terms of input and output type signature), and what are the type signatures of the functions given to you - may help you quickly find the best way to combine the given functions (or some of them) to arrive at your goal of implementing the desired function / transformation.

For instance (as a matter of reverse engineering) - think of a function that takes in a List of Strings and delivers the sum of their lengths. The type of this function should be List[String] => Int. Now getting the length can be done through application of the *length* function on Strings. So *length* is of type *String => Int*. And the *sum* function applicable to a *List[Int]* should be of type *List[Int] => Int*, as it converts a List[Int] to an Int.

So we need a function -

totalLengthOfStrings : List[String] => Int

and we are given

length : String => Int

and

sum : List[Int] => Int

(Note that the input type for the function to be implemented is also given, in the sense that this will be the starting point of the whole operation.)

Now following the types we can try to derive the way to combine the given functions (to get the desired one) as follows -

List[String] map (String => Int) provides List[Int]

List[Int] transformed through (List[Int] => Int) provides Int

or in a somewhat notational way (note that this is not a standard notation, but I am using it as my own convention, but this could be useful, if you get the hang of it. Here <something> means a value of that 'something' type. and <f: some type => other type> means converted through a function of some type => other type. This function may be either an inner function [in which case it will appear appropriately within the parentheses of the outer HOF], or an outer function [in which case it appears without the parentheses]. The notation {some type} means at this point some type is the resultant type for the processing in the pipeline thus far. This helps putting a marker on the intermediate types for easier deduction.)

<List[String]>.map(f: String => Int){List[Int]}.<f: List[Int] => Int> => Int

...

Now note that if you have a List of element type A (List[A]), and you wish to have List[B] from it, and you have a function that takes you from A to B (f: A => B) you can use the map function for your conversion.

<List[A]>.map(f: A => B) => List[B]

If however instead of a function of type A => B, you have a function of type A => List[B], the way to go eventually is flatMap.

<List[A]>.flatMap(f: A => List[B]) => List[B]

Transformations on List (continued...)

'flatMap' is possibly the most important functional transformation after 'map'. It has uses in functional structures like Monad, primarily because it has the natural capability to 'bind' (or plug in) lists hierarchically. This is also made use of in Scala, in providing of *for expression* with multiple generators. [Note that while map and filter can bind lists end to end (and flatMap also has that ability), flatMap can chain lists internally even before producing the final output. E.g. a List of 3 items can be flatMapped to produce 3 Lists (one per item, as the internal function is of general type A => List[B]) and List operations can happen on each of these 3 lists thereafter, and the results of those further operations on the Lists can be combined into a single List by flattening]. The example of for expression below, will hopefully clarify it further.]

...

Note that for expression (also known as *for comprehension*) is an imperative style of construct (sequential). However sometimes, being able to write a piece code in such a style may feel more natural.

Scala provides *for expressions* in many flavours, (more a matter of syntactic sugar to support the 'feel natural' style of coding), and under the hood they may be converted to more functional constructs. For example -

for {

  x <- List(1, 2, 3)

} yield x + 1

(a for comprehension with single generator), will be internally converted to

List(1, 2, 3).map(_ + 1)

and an expression like -

for {

  i <- List('X', 'Y', 'Z')

j <- List(1, 2)

  k <- List('a', 'b', 'c', 'd')

} yield(i, j, k)

      (a for comprehension with multiple generators), will be internally converted to

List('X', 'Y', 'Z').flatMap { i =>

  List(1, 2).flatMap { j =>

   List('a', 'b', 'c', 'd').map { k =>

   (i, j, k)

   }

  }

}

      (Note that all levels except the innermost is flatMap)

      This produces a List of 3-tuples, combining all possible values from each list with other possible combinations from other lists (but keeping the positions of i, j and k intact).

res3: List[(Char, Int, Char)] = List((X,1,a), (X,1,b), (X,1,c), (X,1,d), (X,2,a), (X,2,b), (X,2,c), (X,2,d), (Y,1,a), (Y,1,b), (Y,1,c), (Y,1,d), (Y,2,a), (Y,2,b), (Y,2,c), (Y,2,d), (Z,1,a), (Z,1,b), (Z,1,c), (Z,1,d), (Z,2,a), (Z,2,b), (Z,2,c), (Z,2,d))

      Contrast this with what the result would be if all were maps (at all 3 level)

List('X', 'Y', 'Z').map { i =>

  List(1, 2).map { j =>

   List('a', 'b', 'c', 'd').map { k =>

   (i, j, k)

```
}

}

}
```

This would result in a List of List of List of 3-tuples -

res4: List[List[List[(Char, Int, Char)]]] = List(List(List((X,1,a), (X,1,b), (X,1,c), (X,1,d)), List((X,2,a), (X,2,b), (X,2,c), (X,2,d))), List(List((Y,1,a), (Y,1,b), (Y,1,c), (Y,1,d)), List((Y,2,a), (Y,2,b), (Y,2,c), (Y,2,d))), List(List((Z,1,a), (Z,1,b), (Z,1,c), (Z,1,d)), List((Z,2,a), (Z,2,b), (Z,2,c), (Z,2,d))))

But we really want a flat List of 3 tuples - at least that is what we would expect from a similar nested for in imperative programming. So use of flatMap here - while maintaining the ability of nesting, keeps the level (of Lists) down to a single enclosing List.

Anatomy of foldLeft and flatMap

How could functions like foldLeft and flatMap be implemented from scratch? Using our own non-infix, freestanding version of those functions we could put the signatures as -

def myfoldLeft[A,B](l: List[A], z: B)(op: (B, A) => B): B

def myflatMap[A,B](l: List[A])(f: A => List[B]): List[B]

The following implementation for foldLeft (myfoldLeft) should work -

@annotation.tailrec

def myfoldLeft[A,B](l: List[A], z: B)(op: (B, A) => B): B = l match {

* case h :: t => myfoldLeft(t, op(z,h))(op)*

* case Nil => z*

}

For myflatMap however the following implementation -

```scala
def myflatMap[A,B](l: List[A])(f: A => List[B]): List[B] = l match {
  case h :: t => f(h) ::: myflatMap(t)(f)
  case Nil => Nil
}
```

will not be *tail recursive*. For a *tail recursive* version, we can use the trick of inner function and passing accumulated ListBuffer as a parameter to that function (as was the case in map).

```scala
def myflatMap[A,B](l: List[A])(f: A => List[B]): List[B] = {
  import scala.collection.mutable.ListBuffer


  val acc = ListBuffer[B]()


  @annotation.tailrec
  def go(lst: List[A], fn: A => List[B], acc:ListBuffer[B]): List[B] = lst match {
    case h :: t => go(t, fn, acc ++ fn(h))
    case Nil => acc.toList
  }


  go(l, f, acc)
}
```

You can test the functions with the following statements -

```scala
println("sum List(1,2,3) : " + myfoldLeft(List(1,2,3),0)(_ + _))
```

```
println("flatMap of List(\"l\", \"go\", \"home\") : " +
myflatMap(List("l", "go", "home"))(_.toList))
```

more predicate based transformations
'filter' by no means is the only transformation which processes elements based on a predicate (a function that takes an element and returns a Boolean). There are many more.

You can 'drop' a given number of elements from the beginning of a List, or 'take' a given number of elements (but this is not predicate based).

```
scala> val x = List(1,2,3,4,5,6)

x: List[Int] = List(1, 2, 3, 4, 5, 6)


scala> val y = x.take(5)

y: List[Int] = List(1, 2, 3, 4, 5)


scala> val z = y.drop(2)

z: List[Int] = List(3, 4, 5)
```

takeWhile and dropWhile
If you want similar operation predicate based, you can use *dropWhile* and *takeWhile* (both of which takes predicate rather than Int)

```
scala> val a = x.takeWhile(_ < 6)

a: List[Int] = List(1, 2, 3, 4, 5)


scala> val b = x.dropWhile(_ < 3)
```

b: List[Int] = List(3, 4, 5, 6)

Note that both of them stops once and for all (on the first element that fails). Unlike *filter*, which traverses through the whole List.

scala> val x = List(1, 2, 3, 2, 1)

x: List[Int] = List(1, 2, 3, 2, 1)

scala> val a = x.dropWhile(_ < 3)

a: List[Int] = List(3, 2, 1)

scala> val b = x.takeWhile(_ < 3)

b: List[Int] = List(1, 2)

partition
If you wish to divide a List into two, *with elements with have's and elements with have not's,* you can use partition. This traverses the whole List, so you won't lose any element.

scala> val x = List(1, 2, 3, 4, 0, 2)

x: List[Int] = List(1, 2, 3, 4, 0, 2)

scala> x.partition(_ > 2)

res1: (List[Int], List[Int]) = (List(3, 4),List(1, 2, 0, 2))

It returns a pair (2-tuple) of Lists. The first of which contains the elements (of original List) which satisfies the criteria, and the second one contains the other elements.

Lazy traversal

'withFilter' on a List, is a transformation which allows 'lazy traversal' or traversal with lazy evaluation. It is also a soft filtering. It does 'lazy traversal' in the sense that it does not work on the whole list at once, rather it passes through / or restricts a particular element when a subsequent map (among other things) comes to processing that element. [Thus going through elements one by one as and when they are demanded in subsequent non-lazy transformation (certain type of transformations as given below) in the pipeline]. It is soft filtering in the sense that it does not itself output a concrete List of elements (unlike filter), but rather narrows the domain/scope of operation for subsequent processing (for valid subsequent methods) - by as if labelling (although actually not altering any element) the elements with haves and have not's (which is then - as if - seen by the subsequent process, and is picked up or not picked up for processing).

Perhaps it is best explained with an example. But prior to that, some official documentation would help -

withFilter 'Creates a non-strict filter of this traversable collection. Note: the difference between `c filter p` and `c withFilter p` is that the former creates a new collection, whereas the latter only restricts the domain of subsequent map, flatMap, foreach, and withFilter operations.'

Now for the example - suppose you have a predicate (with *println* so that you know when it is executing) like -

def isGtFour(i: Int): Boolean = {

 println("checking if " + i + " is > 4")

 i > 4

}

and a list like below -

val lst = List(2, 3, 5, 6, 1, 8, 7)

if you run filter on it, all the elements are evaluated one by one and you get a concrete List as output.

scala> val a = lst.filter(isGtFour(_))

checking if 2 is > 4

checking if 3 is > 4

checking if 5 is > 4

checking if 6 is > 4

checking if 1 is > 4

checking if 8 is > 4

checking if 7 is > 4

a: List[Int] = List(5, 6, 8, 7)

If however you invoke *withFilter*, nothing is immediately printed from the predicate [so it is not being immediately run].

scala> val b = lst.withFilter(isGtFour(_))

b: scala.collection.generic.FilterMonadic[Int, List[Int]] = scala.collection.TraversableLike$WithFilter@36e690a7

Now if you call a map on the result of the original filter -

scala> val c = a.map(_ - 2)

c: List[Int] = List(3, 4, 6, 5)

it does not call the predicate function any more, and works on a list of 4 items as expected.

If a similar map is called on the result of *withFilter*, then it is rather different story.

scala> val d = b.map(_ - 2)

checking if 2 is > 4

checking if 3 is > 4

checking if 5 is > 4

checking if 6 is > 4

checking if 1 is > 4

checking if 8 is > 4

checking if 7 is > 4

d: List[Int] = List(3, 4, 6, 5)

Note that if you were to apply another *withFilter*, with a different predicate in series, the second predicate would only be called for the elements that makes through the first predicate. Suppose we have a second predicate -

def isLtSeven(i: Int): Boolean = {

  println("checking if " + i + " is < 7")

  i < 7

}

and we try -

scala> val e = b.withFilter(isLtSeven(_))

e: scala.collection.generic.FilterMonadic[Int,List[Int]] = scala.collection.TraversableLike$WithFilter@6oaf64eb

and then -

scala> val f = e.map(_ - 2)

checking if 2 is > 4

checking if 3 is > 4

checking if 5 is > 4

checking if 5 is < 7

checking if 6 is > 4

checking if 6 is < 7

checking if 1 is > 4

checking if 8 is > 4

checking if 8 is < 7

checking if 7 is > 4

checking if 7 is < 7

f: List[Int] = List(3, 4)

Notice that the predicate firing, started only at the map, and the second predicate did not fire for all the elements of the original List. Also note that for the whole withFilter channel (two withFilter together in this case), it is picking up one element from the original List - passing it through the whole filtering channel (as far as it would go), and being done with it prior to picking up the next element.

Now let's move on to something a little different. How to combine two lists element-wise.

zip

zip function combines two list element-wise, and makes a single list of pairs.

If you have two lists like -

val lst1 = List(1,2,3,4)

val lst2 = List("a", "b", "c", "d")

they can be zipped like -

scala> val a = lst1.zip(lst2)

a: List[(Int, String)] = List((1,a), (2,b), (3,c), (4,d))

Note that the lists need not be of same type of elements,

nor they need to be of same length. For differing lengths they are paired up to the length of the smaller List, the remaining elements of bigger List are discarded -

scala> val b = List(1, 2).zip(List("a", "b", "c"))

b: List[(Int, String)] = List((1,a), (2,b))

scala> val c = List(1, 2, 3).zip(List("a", "b"))

c: List[(Int, String)] = List((1,a), (2,b))

zipWithIndex
This is an easy way of indexing the elements of a given List, and could sometimes come very handy.

For a List like -

val lst2 = List("a", "b", "c", "d")

this transformation would work as -

scala> val d = lst2.zipWithIndex

d: List[(String, Int)] = List((a,0), (b,1), (c,2), (d,3))

If you wanted to turn the indexes, thus produced, into the keys of a corresponding Map, whose values would be elements of the original List, you could do the following -

scala> val m = d.toMap.map(_.swap)

m: scala.collection.immutable.Map[Int,String] = Map(0 -> a, 1 -> b, 2 -> c, 3 -> d)

grouping
A List can be grouped into multiple sublists based on a given group size. The 'grouped' function returns an Iterator on

the groups, which further needs to be converted to a List (if you want a List of Lists).

If you have a List like -

val lst = List(1, 2, 3, 4, 5, 6)

The following works -

scala> val a = lst.grouped(3).toList

a: List[List[Int]] = List(List(1, 2, 3), List(4, 5, 6))

If the original List length is not a multiple of the group size, the last List takes up the remaining smaller number of elements.

scala> val b = List(1, 2, 3, 4, 5, 6, 7, 8).grouped(3).toList

b: List[List[Int]] = List(List(1, 2, 3), List(4, 5, 6), List(7, 8))

...

A more useful grouping is based on criteria which groups the sublists into a map with the keys relating to individual criteria values.

Suppose you have a List of 2-tuples with fruits and their colours as below -

val fruits = List(("banana", "yellow"), ("apple", "red"), ("mango", "Yellow"), ("grape", "green"),

("pomegranate","red"),("berry", "blue"),("guava","green"))

You can group the List into a Map of sublists based on the fruit colour (using groupBy function)

scala> val colourGroup = fruits.groupBy(_._2)

colourGroup: scala.collection.immutable.Map[String,List[(String, String)]] = Map(Yellow -> List((mango, Yellow)), blue -> List((berry,blue)), green -> List((grape,green), (guava,green)), yellow -> List((banana,yellow)), red -> List((apple,red), (pomegranate,red)))

This particular function has wide use in map-reduce algorithm (strategy?) in BigData processing. But before discussing that, let's us discuss about 'reduce'.

reduce

This is an aggregating category function (somewhat like fold). This is actually inherited in List from further up the hierarchy. There are a few forms (such as reduceLeft etc.). The plane form has the signature -

def reduce[A1 >: A](op: (A1, A1) => A1): A1

where op is a binary (associative) combining operation. And the List should not be empty.

Note that unlike fold, it does not have an initial element (z) and also the operation takes two arguments of same type (type of elements to be combined), there is no separate compact type (like B in case of foldLeft) involved.

A very simple example would be for a List like -

val c = List(1, 2, 3, 4, 5, 6, 7, 8)

scala> val sum = c.reduce(_ + _)

sum: Int = 36

Note that for types where the combining type and output type are same (and the operation is associative), this is a simpler way of combining than foldLeft. [more typical use case for foldLeft is when you are folding on to a different type with a starting value]. Now to get down to map-reduce.

map-reduce

If you are somewhat familiar with BigData processing

you might have heard of the *map-reduce* technique.

(Typically) this is a functional processing pipeline consisting of -

(a) application of the functions 'map' to transform the input records into records with more essential (transformed) elements for the processing ,

(b) then grouping on the mapped records, through the 'groupBy' function, for ease of summarising,

(c) and then reducing (mapping through a 'reduce' function) on the grouped values, in order to actually summarise the groups, and achieve the target result.

(So ideally it should have been named map-groupBy-reduce, but map-reduce will do for now.)

In practical cases it happens on a possibly huge List of records (usually broken down into multiple smaller List of records, and initially using possibly multiple machines for the map phase at least). Nevertheless, even a small set of data can be worked through, using the same principle.

It's suitability of application in BigData processing comes from the fact that [credit to FP], each stage of processing need not happen in the same machine. And typically the earlier stages of processing (especially 'map') happens on a much larger data volume (than 'reduce') - and the input to map can be segmented into multiple chunks, and each chunk can run on a separate non-expensive computer, and the result can - at one stage - be gathered into a smaller number of machines (or a single machine), and final stages can occur there. This is possible - because in a completely referentially transparent programming architecture, the result of mapping - whether calculated on a single machine or on multiple machines, should have exact same accuracy. [And hence from accuracy point of view either way is ok, but distributed processing helps with the computing load (management) and overall timespan of the process.]

Note that at the mapping stage, output should be same in number as the input, and each entry of the result of mapping is independent of the others (and hence completely distributable). Grouping ideally depends on each other, but it is possible to group through chunks of mapping result, and letter merge the groups, if necessary, in turn - like folding (which [i.e. grouping from the group results of chunks] would not be as expensive compared to grouping the whole lot together).

After grouping part is complete, the resultant data volume would usually be much less compared to the original input data, and would likely be manageable on a single machine.

...

Now getting down to illustration.

Suppose you have a set of files each of which contains records of a survey (taken countrywide from adults who can vote). Suppose each record (each line in those files, comma separated format [CSV]) contains the data for name, age, state(code), postcode, and a string representing political preference. Somewhat like -

Edward,48,QLD,4079,undecided

Cory,66,WA,6012,capitalist

Lawrence,68,TAS,7001,unionist

Given how each of the possible string for preferences (e.g. capitalist, socialist, conservative) maps to one of a few given preference types (such as - Undecided, Liberal, SocialDemocrat) -

the task is to find the count of preferences of the given preference types, amongst the following age groups 18 - 25, 26 -

35, 36 - 45, 46 - 60, above 60. This result can eventually be easily translated to percentage preferences amongst age groups.

For the sake of convenience let's suppose we have two files - *survey1.txt* and *survey2.txt* with 20 records each (as given below).

survey1.txt :

Edward,48,QLD,4079,undecided

Cory,66,WA,6012,capitalist

Lawrence,68,TAS,7001,unionist

Doyle,25,SA,5112,conservative tilt

Purvi,57,WA,6089,nothing in particular

Andy,82,ACT,2605,not decided

Asmi,33,ACT,2610,liberal

Noel,42,QLD,4000,communism

Buba,51,SA,5139,social democrat

Carol,60,TAS,7036,conservative

Richard,34,NSW,2135,socialist

Bernie,73,NSW,2112,communist

Justin,63,SA,5002,free market supporter

Ria,18,VIC,3024,communist

Claire,72,VIC,3113,unionist

Turner,76,VIC,3012,capitalist

Katy,56,TAS,7082,liberal

Keller,19,QLD,4180,socialist

Aaron,36,TAS,7002,social democrat

Kirti,62,ACT,2600,conservative

survey2.txt :

Kora,64,SA,5005,conservative tilt

Christopher,86,QLD,4225,undecided

Keira,52,WA,6013,nothing in particular

Sabina,87,NSW,2541,free market supporter

Logi,40,NSW,2000,not decided

Roberta,21,QLD,4148,communism

Richa,32,WA,6124,undecided

Sarah,39,VIC,3007,communist

Roland,74,VIC,3145,free market supporter

Koni,49,WA,6023,socialist

Peter,54,ACT,2618,communism

Santiago,83,NSW,2144,capitalist

Purvi,50,ACT,2901,nothing in particular

Claire,77,TAS,7114,conservative tilt

Roland,81,SA,5013,conservative

Richard,45,NSW,2541,unionist

Logi,27,WA,6013,social democrat

Roberta,61,QLD,4000,liberal

Turner,58,TAS,7114,not decided

Aaron,80,ACT,2605,social democrat

Note that for the final analysis, we do not need name. Just the preference (classified), and the age-group the voter belongs to. So we can run mapping to get those data from each record of those two files. We can run each file on a separate machine. [For exercise purposes similar mapping program can be run on two different input files, in the same machine, to generate two different output files.]

For the mapping part the following program should work (which takes the input and output filenames as runtime argument) [the program file is named *mapit.scala*]-

import java.io.PrintWriter

import java.io.File

import scala.io.Source

case class Rec(name:String, age:Int, state:String, postcode:Int, opinion:String)

object Mapit {

def recLst(inFile: String): List[Rec] = (for (line <- Source.fromFile(inFile).getLines)

yield(line.split(",") match { case Array(a,b,c,d,e) => Rec(a, b.toInt, c, d.toInt, e) })

).toList

def polClassify(rec: Rec): (String, String) = {

val pol = rec.opinion match {

```scala
    case "not decided" | "undecided" | "nothing in particular" =>
"Undecided"
    case "socialist" | "social democrat" | "communist" | "unionist" =>
"SocialDemocrat"
    case "conservative" | "liberal" | "free market supporter" =>
"Liberal"
    }


    //18 - 25, 26 - 35, 36 - 45, 46 - 60, above 60
    val ageGrp =
      if (rec.age >= 18 && rec.age <= 25) "18 - 25"
      else if (rec.age >= 26 && rec.age <= 35) "26 - 35"
      else if (rec.age >= 36 && rec.age <= 45) "36 - 45"
      else if (rec.age >= 46 && rec.age <= 60) "46 - 60"
      else "above 60"


    (ageGrp, pol)
  }


  def main(args: Array[String]): Unit = {
    val inFile = args(0)
    val outFile = args(1)
    val writer = new PrintWriter(new File(outFile))
    recLst(inFile).map(polClassify(_)).foreach(t => writer.write(t._1 +
"," + t._2 + "\n"))
```

```
    writer.close

  }


}


Mapit.main(Array("survey1.txt", "mapped1.txt"))

Mapit.main(Array("survey2.txt", "mapped2.txt"))
```

Note that this is a rather simple mapping, classifying the opinion (Strings) into particular labels and the age into particular age groups (Strings).

This should create two mapped files *mapped1.txt* and *mapped2.txt* with output records -

mapped1.txt :

46 - 60,Liberal

above 60,SocialDemocrat

above 60,Undecided

18 - 25,SocialDemocrat

46 - 60,SocialDemocrat

above 60,SocialDemocrat

26 - 35,Undecided

36 - 45,Liberal

46 - 60,Undecided

46 - 60,Liberal

26 - 35,Liberal

above 60, Undecided

above 60, SocialDemocrat

18 - 25, SocialDemocrat

above 60, Liberal

above 60, Undecided

46 - 60, SocialDemocrat

18 - 25, Undecided

36 - 45, SocialDemocrat

above 60, Liberal

mapped2.txt :

above 60, Undecided

above 60, Undecided

46 - 60, Liberal

above 60, Liberal

36 - 45, SocialDemocrat

18 - 25, SocialDemocrat

26 - 35, Undecided

36 - 45, Liberal

above 60, SocialDemocrat

46 - 60, SocialDemocrat

46 - 60, Undecided

above 60, SocialDemocrat

46 - 60, SocialDemocrat

above 60, SocialDemocrat

above 60, SocialDemocrat

36 - 45, Liberal

26 - 35, Undecided

above 60, Liberal

46 - 60, Liberal

above 60, Undecided

As you can see the data volume to be processed further is already much less. At this point the processing can take one of three ways

(1) Take the mapped data (merged) in one machine and run grouping and reduce on that

(2) Merge the mapped data into fewer files and run grouping and reduce in each of them and then merge the result (through further grouping and reduce on the individual results of grouping and reduce, produced by these machines.)

(3) Do the grouping and reduce on each mapped dataset (on perhaps the same set of machines), and merge the results of these grouping and reduction - using further (almost similar) grouping and reduction.

So broadly it is either (a) a single stage grouping and reduce on the merged map data. Or (b) grouping and reduce on multiple sets of mapped data - merge them - and further grouping and reduce on the merged grouped and reduced data. Of these (b) is more general approach. So approach (b) is better (more generic) topic of discussion. Processing with approach (a) is covered in the processing with approach (b) trivially. [When the first stage of (b) involves the complete mapped file as input, that stage itself constitutes the entire (a) approach]

...

So our aim is to - (1) separately run grouping and reduce on the two mapped files. (2) merge the files (simple concatenation) (3) run further grouping and reduce on the merged (grouped and reduced) dataset. [Note that for this second phase of grouping and reduce, the input record will be in a different shape than the mapped data].

The step (2) above is simple concatenation. The steps (1) and (3) can both be catered by the following program [with slight commenting uncommenting] -

import java.io.PrintWriter

import java.io.File

import scala.io.Source

case class Grp(ageGrp: String, pref: String)

case class Mapped(grp: Grp, count:Int)

object Grpred {

def recLst(inFile: String): List[Mapped] = (for (line <- Source.fromFile(inFile).getLines)

yield(line.split(",") match {

case Array(a,b) => Mapped(Grp(a,b),1)

case Array(a,b,c) => Mapped(Grp(a,b),c.toInt)

})

).toList

```scala
def combine(a: Mapped, b:Mapped) = {
  if (a.grp == b.grp) Mapped(a.grp, a.count + b.count)
  else throw new Exception("Can't combine dissimilar groups")
}


def main(args: Array[String]): Unit = {
  val inFile = args(0)
  val outFile = args(1)
  val grpCounts =
recLst(inFile).groupBy(_.grp).values.map(_.reduce(combine(_, _)))
  val writer = new PrintWriter(new File(outFile))
  grpCounts.foreach(t => writer.write(t.grp.ageGrp + "," +
t.grp.pref + "," + t.count + "\n"))
  writer.close
}

}


Grpred.main(Array("mapped1.txt", "rslt1.txt"))
Grpred.main(Array("mapped2.txt", "rslt2.txt"))
//Grpred.main(Array("rslt.txt", "final.txt"))
```

Note that of the two cases in the *recLst* method, the first case applies to the mapped data as input (step (1)), and the second case applies to the grouped and reduced data as input (step (3)).

Note also the *combine* function which is the inner function for *reduce* - takes two mapped records and combines their counts (by adding the two), and producing another mapped type record [which will be used as one of the input for combination, with the next record in the List]. 'reduce' is a lot like folding.

Note also that *groupBy* produces a *Map*, each of whose values are a List of records. So the function *values* on the *groupBy(_.grp)* produces a List of Lists (of records). So the map function on that - is a way of getting individual List of records (pertaining to individual age groups for the input dataset) from the List of Lists (of records). These individual List of Records are then reduced through the 'reduce' function into a single record (containing count for the given grouping key in question). Our grouping key is of type Grp, which is a combination of age-group and political opinion (classified few). So we get the count for each distinct combination of age-group and classified political opinion present in the input dataset.

When two such grouped and counted result-sets are merged, the merged groups would be a set union of the original groups. In such merger, repetition of existing combinations will be again grouped and reduced (summed) to give rise to a single overall count for the grouping key (grouping combination).

Grouping and reducing through the individual mapped files (mapped1.txt and mapped2.txt) in our example, should produce two result files -

rslt1.txt:

26 - 35,Liberal,1

36 - 45,SocialDemocrat,1

above 60,Undecided,3

46 - 60,Liberal,2

above 60,SocialDemocrat,3

26 - 35,Undecided,1

18 - 25,SocialDemocrat,2

46 - 60,SocialDemocrat,2

18 - 25,Undecided,1

above 60,Liberal,2

36 - 45,Liberal,1

46 - 60,Undecided,1

rslt2.txt:

36 - 45,SocialDemocrat,1

above 60,Undecided,3

46 - 60,Liberal,2

above 60,SocialDemocrat,4

26 - 35,Undecided,2

18 - 25,SocialDemocrat,1

46 - 60,SocialDemocrat,2

above 60,Liberal,2

36 - 45,Liberal,2

46 - 60,Undecided,1

and a plane concatenation of those files, (into a file named *rslt.txt*) and running the grouping and reduction on that [need to comment the first two calls to main, and uncomment the last call] should produce the final counts.

finale.txt:

26 - 35, Liberal, 1

36 - 45, SocialDemocrat, 2

above 60, Undecided, 6

46 - 60, Liberal, 4

above 60, SocialDemocrat, 7

26 - 35, Undecided, 3

18 - 25, SocialDemocrat, 3

46 - 60, SocialDemocrat, 4

18 - 25, Undecided, 1

above 60, Liberal, 4

36 - 45, Liberal, 3

46 - 60, Undecided, 2

    ...

At a glance it appears that the SocialDemocrats are a majority.

Functional transformation – a demonstration

We are drawing towards the close of our discussion on functional transformation on Lists. Note that extensive functional transformations on other data structures - notably Maps and Sets - are also possible. But hopefully, a good coverage of the topic on Lists, has given a good taste of what it is about.

Quiet a few transformations on List has been discussed (although there are many more). The following case study makes good use of many of the transformations, and (hopefully) provides a good clue as to how they may be put together, to reach a target result set, from a given collection of input data.

The task is as follows.

[Take a fictitious case.] Suppose someone (say John) has a credit card, for himself and two subsidiary cards (used by his wife and son). You have been given an expense file for the expenses incurred through these 3 cards for a month.

expense.txt:

101,25-01-2017,groceries,56.80

101,26-01-2017,petrol,34.50

101,27-01-2017,phone bill,35.40

101,30-01-2017,coffee,3.70

101,31-01-2017,salon,25.50

102,03-01-2017,fish and chips,9.75

102,04-01-2017,rice and fish curry,14.65

102,05-01-2017,Pizzo veg pizza,8.50

102,06-01-2017,fish and chips,9.75

102,09-01-2017,rice and veg. curry,11.50

102,10-01-2017,chicken burger and drink,9.80

102,11-01-2017,Pizzo chicken pizza,12.50

102,11-01-2017,groceries,24.00

102,12-01-2017,fish and chips,9.75

102,13-01-2017,rice and fish curry,14.65

102,17-01-2017,Pizzo chicken pizza,12.50

102,18-01-2017,fish and chips,9.75

102,18-01-2017,medicine,13.75

102,19-01-2017,rice and fish curry,14.65

102,20-01-2017,Pizzo veg pizza,8.50

102,23-01-2017,fish and chips,9.75

102,24-01-2017,seafood platter,16.45

102,25-01-2017,Pizzo veg pizza,8.50

102,26-01-2017,fish and chips,9.75

102,27-01-2017,rice and veg. curry,11.50

102,30-01-2017,fish and chips,9.75

102,31-01-2017,chicken burger and drink,9.80

103,03-01-2017,school canteen,6.50

103,04-01-2017,remote controlled car,25.00

103,05-01-2017,cricket balls,6.45

103,06-01-2017,stationary,9.75

103,09-01-2017,chicken burger,7.80

The fields are account number, date, description and expense in that order.

John's account number is 102. And the reporting for the month in the form of date description and expenses are to be prepared for his food expenses only. Somewhat like -

03-01-2017,fish and chips,9.75

04-01-2017,rice and fish curry,14.65

05-01-2017,Pizzo veg pizza,8.5

...

But there are few catches. For each purchase of Pizzo

pizzas, he gets a 20% discount which has to be recorded (as negative amounts - because it is expense report). For every fourth purchase of fish and chips, he gets full cash back (although the initial charge occurs on credit card - this helps him with frequent flyer points). So those entries of fish and chips (every fourth one), are to be omitted from report.

Besides, expenses for *medicine* and *groceries* are to be omitted also (because it is an expense report related to food expenses).

...

Let's see how individual problems can be tackled. [For each code fragments given below, assume appropriate supporting code, e.g. required imports, case classes etc., even if not shown, are in fact, in place.]

Firstly we can have two case classes purely based on input data format, and output format required.

case class Txn(acctNo: Int, dt: String, dtl: String, amt: Double)

case class Rpt(dt: String, dtl: String, amt: String)

The reading of the input data rows (into a List of Txn) can be done with a function like -

def txnLst: List[Txn] = (

for (line <- Source.fromFile("expense.txt").getLines)

  yield(line.split(",") match {case Array(a,b,c,d) => Txn(a.toInt, b, c, d.toDouble)})

).toList

[expense.txt file is in the same directory (in a properly organized project, it can be appropriately placed in the path)]

For a Txn which will be straightaway reported, we can have a function to map a *Txn* to an *Rpt*.

```
def toRpt(txn: Txn): Rpt = Rpt(txn.dt, txn.dtl,
"%.02f".format(txn.amt))
```

...

For Pizzo pizza transactions, each one will generate two rows in the report (*List[Rpt]*). From one *Txn* to a *List[Rpt]*, looks like a case for flatMap. A function like this can do the conversion of individual Txns (the inner function of flatMap).

```
def breakDown(txn: Txn): List[Rpt] =

 List(

  Rpt(txn.dt, txn.dtl, "%.02f".format(txn.amt)),

  Rpt(txn.dt, txn.dtl + " discount", "%.02f".format(txn.amt * -
0.20))

 )
```

...

Now to get down to actual Txns for account number 102, notice that the rows are grouped together, per account in the input file. So we can keep dropping until we reach txns for account 102, and then keep taking so long as it is 102 txns.

That gives us -

```
txnLst.dropWhile(_.acctNo != 102).takeWhile(_.acctNo == 102)
```

But on top of that we need to discard medicine and groceries (which calls for filtering) so -

```
txnLst.dropWhile(_.acctNo != 102).takeWhile(_.acctNo == 102)

 .filter(_.dtl != "groceries").filter(_.dtl != "medicine")
```

At this stage we have our transactions of interest. But we need to eat away every fourth fish and chips record (figuratively speaking). So we should handle them parallely to other transactions. A 'partition'ing will be handy.

```
val (fishAndChipsLst, others) = txnLst.dropWhile(_.acctNo !=
102).takeWhile(_.acctNo == 102)
```

```
.filter(_.dtl != "groceries").filter(_.dtl != "medicine")
```

```
.partition(_.dtl == "fish and chips")
```

...

At this point we should have all fish and chips transactions in a neat List, and other transactions of interest in another list.

In order to find every fourth fish and chips transactions, we can zip it with index, so that it is easy to recognize and deal with 4th transactions.

```
fishAndChipsLst.zipWithIndex
```

```
.filter(t => (((t._2 + 1) % 4) != 0))
```

Once such transactions are filtered out, we can take the rest of zipped transactions [of which the first of the tuple is the actual transaction, and the second it's index], and map them to Rpts.

```
fishAndChipsLst.zipWithIndex
```

```
.filter(t => (((t._2 + 1) % 4) != 0))
```

```
.map {t => toRpt(t._1)}
```

That takes care of putting relevant fish and chips transactions into Rpts. Now think about the other transactions.

The only type here that require special handling (breaking down into two Rpt) are the Pizzo transactions.

```
others.flatMap { t =>
```

```
t.dtl.substring(0,5) match {
```

```
case "Pizzo" => breakDown(t)
```

...

The rest should be mapped directly to Rpts. So we have -

```
others.flatMap { t =>
  t.dtl.substring(0,5) match {
    case "Pizzo" => breakDown(t)
    case _ => List(toRpt(t))
  }
}
```

...

After all this is done, we would be left with two List of Rpts. But we have to deliver only one, which should be the concatenation of these two Lists. So -

```
val rptLst: List[Rpt] = (
  fishAndChipsLst.zipWithIndex
    .filter(t => (((t._2 + 1) % 4) != 0))
    .map {t => toRpt(t._1)} ++
  others.flatMap { t =>
    t.dtl.substring(0,5) match {
      case "Pizzo" => breakDown(t)
      case _ => List(toRpt(t))
    }
  }
).sortBy(_.dt)
```

The sorting by dt (date) for the Rpts (reports) are to be done to get the concatenated List sorted by date.

So we have used - *map, flatMap, filter, dropWhile, takeWhile, partition,* and *zipWithIndex*. The final shape of the solution is -

import scala.io.Source

import java.io.PrintWriter

import java.io.File

case class Txn(acctNo: Int, dt: String, dtl: String, amt: Double)

case class Rpt(dt: String, dtl: String, amt: String)

object Exp {

def writeLst(rptLst: List[Rpt], outFile: String) : Unit = {

val writer = new PrintWriter(new File(outFile))

rptLst.foreach(rpt => writer.write(rpt.dt + "," + rpt.dtl + "," + rpt.amt + "\n"))

writer.close

}

def main(args: Array[String]) = {

writeLst(foodExpRpt(txnLst), "rpt.txt")

}

def txnLst: List[Txn] = (

for (line <- Source.fromFile("expense.txt").getLines)

```
      yield(line.split(",") match {case Array(a,b,c,d) =>
Txn(a.toInt, b, c, d.toDouble)})
      ).toList


//for flatMap
def breakDown(txn: Txn): List[Rpt] =
 List(
  Rpt(txn.dt, txn.dtl, "%.02f".format(txn.amt)),
  Rpt(txn.dt, txn.dtl + " discount", "%.02f".format(txn.amt * -
0.20))
 )


 def toRpt(txn: Txn): Rpt = Rpt(txn.dt, txn.dtl,
"%.02f".format(txn.amt))


 def foodExpRpt(txnLst: List[Txn]): List[Rpt] = {


 val (fishAndChipsLst, others) = txnLst.dropWhile(_.acctNo !=
102).takeWhile(_.acctNo == 102)
  .filter(_.dtl != "groceries").filter(_.dtl != "medicine")
  .partition(_.dtl == "fish and chips")


 val rptLst: List[Rpt] = (
 fishAndChipsLst.zipWithIndex
  .filter(t => (((t._2 + 1) % 4) != 0))
```

```
    .map {t => toRpt(t._1)} ++
  others.flatMap { t =>
    t.dtl.substring(0,5) match {
      case "Pizzo" => breakDown(t)
      case _ => List(toRpt(t))
    }
  }
).sortBy(_.dt)

  rptLst
}
}


Exp.main(Array())
```

And the output is -

rpt.txt:

03-01-2017,fish and chips,9.75

04-01-2017,rice and fish curry,14.65

05-01-2017,Pizzo veg pizza,8.50

05-01-2017,Pizzo veg pizza discount,-1.70

06-01-2017,fish and chips,9.75

09-01-2017,rice and veg. curry,11.50

10-01-2017,chicken burger and drink,9.80

11-01-2017,Pizzo chicken pizza,12.50

11-01-2017,Pizzo chicken pizza discount,-2.50

12-01-2017,fish and chips,9.75

13-01-2017,rice and fish curry,14.65

17-01-2017,Pizzo chicken pizza,12.50

17-01-2017,Pizzo chicken pizza discount,-2.50

19-01-2017,rice and fish curry,14.65

20-01-2017,Pizzo veg pizza,8.50

20-01-2017,Pizzo veg pizza discount,-1.70

23-01-2017,fish and chips,9.75

24-01-2017,seafood platter,16.45

25-01-2017,Pizzo veg pizza,8.50

25-01-2017,Pizzo veg pizza discount,-1.70

26-01-2017,fish and chips,9.75

27-01-2017,rice and veg. curry,11.50

30-01-2017,fish and chips,9.75

31-01-2017,chicken burger and drink,9.80

Totalling the expenses for the month, if you have the rptLst handy, should be a trivial exercise.

...

This is as far as we go in our present journey of functional transformations on Lists. The next chapter discusses some exception handling FP way.

Exception handling – functional way

"Extinction is the rule. Survival is the exception."

- Carl Sagan

Exceptions are an inevitable part of programming. And Handling exceptions, an inevitable part of good programming.

But why should it need special attention in functional programming (as opposed to doing it the same way as in imperative programming)? Why do you need to talk about it in context of FP?

Well, (1) it breaks Referential Transparency (you can not rely completely on substitution - with the same confidence that you can say 1 + 2 + 3 can always be substituted with 6), and (2) it is not type safe.

Consider the following functions -

scala> def excp1(): Int = { throw new Exception("In place of Int") }

excp1: ()Int

scala> def excp2(): String = { throw new Exception("In place of String") }

excp2: ()String

It appears that Exception takes on any colour (in a manner of speaking) that you want it to take on. And that is not good for type checking.

Matter of return type surprise : When you write a function to return an Int, somebody using this function would ideally be able to count on your returning an Int. If he gets an Exception it is bad, and when he gets an exception in the guise of an Int, it is even worse. Ideally he should be able to call your function, process an Int, and be done with it.

Matter of nesting in call and handling : Note also the fact that, the function which is the immediate caller of your function, may pass the result on as it is to the next level of call (or even pass the function itself), and this passing on may go through a few levels, before finally a level of code, is designed to use the result. For that level, your function is rather deep to know directly anything about. And hence coming to a decision for that level, to handle exception from your function doesn't provide the best level of transparency (to put it mildly).

So what could be the possible alternatives?

One way to go is to raise a sentinel value. (a value or some set of values that indicate the function has resulted in error. For instance Unix shell commands usually return a zero for success of the command and a positive integer on failure). So for a function which is expected to return an Int, you return a specific Int value (say -1) to indicate that an exception has occurred. (So the type safety is not violated)

But it brings in it's own baggage.

(1) Special policy : Your caller needs to be aware that he has to treat some Int value as error condition. Not all Int's are equal. (and that does not sound like type safety).

(2) Boilerplate code : an extra if or case (or something like that), to handle the special case, at any level it is meant to be handled.

(3) Non-existent domain of invalidity : The sentinel value has to be something, that can not be a valid value for normal operation. (Hence reserved for error). If your function can normally return zero or positive integers, you can use a negative

integer as sentinel value. However, think of a function that returns an account balance (and for arguments sake say this account allows for unlimited overdraft). The valid return value could be any Double, positive, zero or negative. The domain of invalidity (invalid values) is non-existent. You do not have a legitimate sentinel (Double) value to indicate error.

(4) Enumerated (or similar) Types : If the type has only very limited values (and all in good use), you don't have a legitimate sentinel value [This is actually somewhat akin to the previous point]. For instance if your function is designed to return a Boolean, and both true and false is a possibility of normal processing, what Boolean value could you return to indicate error?

So you can not get the normal return value to carry the burden of error indication. [Good cop, bad cop routine, has to be played by two different cops.]

...

Any other possibility requires segregation of normal return value with some kind of error indicator. For example - suppose, instead of returning an Int, you return a tuple of (Int, Boolean), where the Int carries the result of successful operation, and the Boolean is true or false, to indicate if the result is to be interpreted as Normal or Exception. This is at least an improvement in terms of delegation through the hierarchy. Even at 5 levels up, another function uses the type, it can use the result, to check the Boolean first and then if ok, use the Int returned (or otherwise take appropriate action).

...

The most common vehicle of Exception Handling type in Scala (which means there are others), known as Option, uses a principle somewhat akin to this (although not exactly the same)

In C language, pointer is a well known concept. Java however talks about reference. The only place Java talks about pointer (in my knowledge) is in NullPointerException. In a lot of processing, when something goes wrong, the supposed to be returned variable does not get assigned any value at all, and the calling function gets a null value. Trying to call a method (say) on this resulting (supposed) object ends in NullPointerException. A lot of boilerplate code (and other code) may go into handling such issue.

Instead if we have a type where the possibility of 'No value at all' is built into the type, this type can be safe as return type from a function. I.e. a function which would normally return an Int, may have a choice of returning a type, which may be either an Int or No value (and similarly a function which would normally return a String, may have a choice of returning a type, which may be either a String or No value), i.e. If we had a general (tuple-ish) type that allows us to mix the 'No value' value with any other Single type - then we have a general solution to a return type that is inclusive of abnormality indicator for any function. [And the caller function also may handle it as that type, so it's handling would be inclusive of No value case]. This type is Option.

Option

In official documentation (latest that I could find in the internet) Option is defined as

sealed abstract class Option[+A] extends Product with Serializable

and described as -

'Represents optional values. Instances of Option are either an instance of scala.Some or the object None.'

Some and None in turn are defined as -

final case class Some[+A](value: A) extends Option[A] with Product with Serializable

object None extends Option[Nothing] with Product with Serializable

...

To simplify it for our purpose (ignoring the parts that we are not interested in), let's put it as -

sealed abstract class Option[+A]

final case class Some[+A](value: A) extends Option[A]

object None extends Option[Nothing]

Which means that Option is a sealed abstract class (and a type constructor like List, and a covariant one at that [like List]).

Being a type constructor, it has to take an inner type to make a complete type. e.g. Option of something such as Option[Int], Option[String], Option[Boolean] etc. The function that would otherwise return an Int (as we discussed earlier) should choose Option[Int] instead as return type, and the function which would otherwise return a String should choose Option[String] as return type. (Remember Option is like the 'tuple-ish' wrapper of one other type plus the exception indicator, that one other type is the inner type here).

Being a sealed abstract class, it can only be instantiated through one of it's given subtypes (one of the two given above). [All subclasses of a sealed class (whether it's abstract or not) must be in the same file as the sealed class. This is in a way making sure, that what all possible direct incarnation it can have (as regards to immediate subclassing) is known at the outset. This, among other things, makes handling an instance of the type through pattern matching (using case for instance) watertight. Because you know these are the only possible cases you need to handle.]

So an Option instance could either be a None (an object) which indicates the No value (and being the no value it can go with any type - because : a box of chocolate should contain chocolate, a box of pen should contain pens, but an empty box does not have to be an empty box of chocolate or an empty box of pen specifically - it is just an empty box)

The other way it can have an instance, (and this part should represent the value of successful processing from the function) is to be Some(of a value of some type) e.g. Some(Int), Some(String) etc. but that type would be the inner type of the Option. So Option[Int] can be either None or Some(an Int value), Option[String] can be either None or Some(a String value) and so on.

...

In short a value of type Option[A] can be either None or Some(a value of type A). *None* indicating no result returned (something like null return but this is not really a Null, but a real object, so still tangible and 'handleable'). And *Some(a)* indicating the process having properly finished resulted in the value *a*.

This would result in a consistent type to pass across from source, and handle at target. The processing function returns an Option[Int] (say), and the client function handles an Option[Int]. Doing one thing with the success value, and another thing when None is found. And this does not change even if the return value is passed in the form of option, through 5 levels of nested calling. There is no separate knowledge required about the particular source of the data (the processing function) and the convention it uses. To be able to handle it, Just knowledge of Options is enough. [Note that this does not express the particular error, only indication of failure (and thereby of success), and the right return value upon success. There are other types, such as Either which has a more detailed take on this (and you can device your own type to deal with things anyway). But most often for the target (client) code, it is enough to know that the value is usable or not. It may not bother about - why particularly it failed, but just that it failed, so that it would take the alternate path. In this sense it is most general (because it is most minimal) of such types.]

Packing and unpacking

Eventually we will have to come down to be able to put values in Option so that they can be passed as return values and be able to enquire them at the target site and get the value out of it, when it exists.

How can we create Options. There is not much issue in that.

scala> val x: Option[Int] = Some(3)

x: Option[Int] = Some(3)

scala> val y: Option[Int] = None

y: Option[Int] = None

scala> x.get

res0: Int = 3

scala> val s1: Option[String] = Some("abcd")

s1: Option[String] = Some(abcd)

scala> val s2: Option[String] = None

s2: Option[String] = None

Simple enough? so if you have a function which can possibly get into divide by zero, how do you go about fashioning the return value (for now assume that we are interested in integer division). You could do it simply like -

def divi(a:Int, b:Int): Option[Int] = if (b == 0) None else Some(a/b)

And based on the kind of parameters you call it with, you may get something like -

scala> val a = divi(3, 2)

a: Option[Int] = Some(1)

scala> val b = divi(2,0)

b: Option[Int] = None

So that's about it as far as creation goes. You either flick a None, or wrap the value of calculation (or the whole expression) in a Some.

How to unpack? The answer is not so simple.

On the above *a* and *b*, if you try calling 'get' (to get the value) this will result in the following -

scala> a.get

res3: Int = 1

scala> b.get

java.util.NoSuchElementException: None.get

  at scala.None$.get(Option.scala:347)

  at scala.None$.get(Option.scala:345)

Fair enough. You can only get the value, if it exists. The idea is not to assume beforehand that it will always have a proper value (as opposed to None). How to go about it?

The Option API is actually quite rich in a lot of transformational methods [a lot of familiar(?) faces including *map, flatMap, filter* and *foldLeft* - to the extent that to a weary traveller, it may suddenly appear like the List API. And the familiarity actually helps a great deal with intuitive insight, as it were, in the way those transformations should behave for an Option]. For any transformation of general nature (such as *map* and *flatMap*), the 'typal' difference being - the List is replaced by Option. For example - *map* on Option, works on an Option[A] (instead of List[A]) using an inner function of type A => B and it's output is of type Option[B]

final def map[B](f: (A) ⇒ B): Option[B]

But there are some unfamiliar faces too. Two very important one's (which are peculiar to Options) being - orElse and getOrElse

final def orElse[B >: A](default: => Option[B]): Option[B]

final def getOrElse[B >: A](default: => B): B

Both of these (not assuming whether the value returned has a proper value or None on the outset), provides a hint on what to do in case the value turns out to be None.

The major difference being, in one case the return type is the target element type (B) and in another case it is Option of the target element type (Option[B]). Note that the default value, intuitively, should be same as the return type, because that way it is easier to pass it as it is for return.

Let's examine how they may help.

```
scala> a.getOrElse(0)

res5: Int = 1
```

```
scala> b.getOrElse(0)

res6: Int = 0
```

The client code has come to a decision that in case the called function returns a None, it will proceed with it's value as zero. hence it passes that as the default value in getOrElse. When there is a proper value, it gets that. Otherwise it gets zero (and not any exception), and proceeds with it's business, without interrupting the control flow.

Good. But what about orElse, why would we need to return another Option, instead of actual value? (when we are already trying to access the value at this point anyway).

This gets a whole lot interesting. Note that processing may not necessarily happen (and quite often does not happen) in a single stage. The database access layer in an application, may try to retrieve a single record from database. Which may, among other things end up in NO_DATA_FOUND or TOO_MANY_ROWS kind of error. In which case (assuming we are talking about Options) you would need to return None (otherwise return a healthy record wrapped in Some). The business processing layer - which uses this value to do further processing - may pick three columns of the whole record. Divide one column by another and multiply the result by 100. Then pass the reduced set of columns (Lets say - as an instance of another class named BonusPercentage) to another frontal layer (to do even further processing). But the business layer also have to pass it as an Option (of BonusPercentage), because when it gets a normal record it can in turn output a proper BonusPercentage instance. But if it gets None from the DAO layer, it has to pass a

None (to do justice to it's own client code).

Thus all intermediate processing in the chain of processing - will typically retrieve from an option, do it's processing and pass an Option in turn (of typically another type), to the next level of processing. In this way, a None from the very first layer can get propagated through to the end, without causing any headache.

In order to support this chaining of intermediate processing, a transformation like orElse comes extremely handy.

Now what is the variance bound [B >: A] doing on orElse and getOrElse.

Note that in Scala you cannot normally have covariant types in method parameters (for reasons of type safety such is restricted). In order to have a covariant types in method parameter, you must use a bounded type. And note also that Option is covariant in it's inner type [+A], hence the type bound is necessary in the definition.

It specifies that the return type of the method (of say getOrElse have to be a super-type [or the same type] as A)

But it does not necessarily mean that you will have to pass a super-type as default consciously. Scala can internally convert the default to a super-type of A, as long as such is possible.

For example - in our previous example of b = divi(2,0), if you were to call the getOrElse on b with a String, then -

scala> b.getOrElse("Could not calculate")

res1: Any = Could not calculate

It infers the default's type as *Any* Instead of *String* (as *Any* is a super-type of *Int*), and thus it makes the return type *Any* in this case.

map and filter

Now remember that the whole backdrop of exception handling is meaningful only in context of processing (that processing sometimes generates exceptions). Without processing, exception handling is meaningless. So how the underlying processing will occur with the inner types that Option is wrapping around and chaining through. One way is to explicitly extract the inner value through pattern matching, and in case of Some, take the value and do whatever processing required. And then wrap the value in another Some for the next level of processing. In case of None, that gets directly passed through to the next level. Would it not be good, if this pattern match need not be done at each function which processes the Option values, and can instead be abstracted. Such abstraction of course is possible. (through functional transformations such as 'map' and 'filter' to name a few).

map in Option has the signature -

final def map[B](f: (A) => B): Option[B]

and filter

final def filter(p: (A) => Boolean): Option[A]

(and does that not look very familiar ?)

Both *map* and *filter* (here) works on an Option, and returns an Option. So they (either of them) may be used appropriately to chain Options in a series (like transformational pipelining of Lists).

Let's see some example of their usage.

with the same definition :

def divi(a:Int, b:Int): Option[Int] = if (b == 0) None else Some(a/b)

val a = divi(3, 2)

val b = divi(2, 0)

Say we try map on *a* and *b*.

*scala> a.map(_ * 2.5)*

res5: Option[Double] = Some(2.5)

*scala> b.map(_ * 2.5)*

res6: Option[Double] = None

We got Option[Double] in either case. And if we filter the result of map -

*scala> a.map(_ * 2.5).filter(_ < 4)*

res9: Option[Double] = Some(2.5)

*scala> a.map(_ * 2.5).filter(_ > 3)*

res10: Option[Double] = None

*scala> b.map(_ * 2.5).filter(_ < 4)*

res11: Option[Double] = None

*scala> b.map(_ * 2.5).filter(_ > 3)*

res12: Option[Double] = None

Hopefully you got the hang of it.

Anatomy of map and filter

While we are at it, let's see how a function like *map* or *filter* on Option, may be written using pattern matching. Here too, we can have our own non-infix version of the functions. The following should do.

def mymap[A,B](optA: Option[A], f: A => B): Option[B] = optA match {

  case Some(a) => Some(f(a))

  case None => None

}

def myfilter[A,B](optA: Option[A], f: A => Boolean): Option[A] = optA match {

  case Some(a) => if (f(a)) Some(a) else None

  case None => None

}

Recursion is not needed as Option only ever has one value.

Note that unlike filter on List, filter here does not reduce number of elements. It just makes an option None, if the predicate evaluates to *false*.

flatMap and fold
Option also has *flatMap* and *foldLeft* functions

The signature of those methods on *Option* class are -

final def flatMap[B](f: (A) => Option[B]): Option[B]

  and

def foldLeft[B](z: B)(op: (B, A) => B): B

Note that Option is returned by a method which is expected (at times) not to return a successful value. This could be because the processing ended in error. But this could also be (especially when in a method, no processing as such is involved, e.g. just returning a value from something) that a value that was to be returned - may be expected not to be available at times (or for different records).

Since the inner function of flatMap should be such a function (returning Option), this can be used to successfully wrap around processing of records, where even when the record itself is available, some of the time one particular field may not have any significant value.

(example of the usage of flatMap may be covered as part of a more elaborate example later on)

...

The concept of *fold* though, is not very meaningful in case of Option. In a *List* you may have multiple items, so aggregating them may be significant. Not so for Options.

This is possibly not in much use, and do not (possibly) have many valid use cases.

A couple of somewhat impractical but valid example would be -

scala> val x: Option[Int] = Some(2)

x: Option[Int] = Some(2)

scala> val y: Option[Int] = None

y: Option[Int] = None

scala> val op1: (String,Int) => String = (b:String, a:Int) => "combined " + b + " " + a

op1: (String, Int) => String = <function2>

```
scala> x.foldLeft("ABCD")(op1)
reso: String = combined ABCD 2
```

```
scala> y.foldLeft("ABCD")(op1)
res1: String = ABCD
```

...

Note that *flatMap* and *map* brings out the inner element of an Option when it is Some(something), otherwise (in None case) it does not do any processing. The difference between the two is that flatMap takes a function that returns an Option, so chaining can happen within flatMap body. So map and flatMap can be used in a similar fashion like in case of Lists, to make a *for comprehension* of multiple generators.

Consider the following example.

Suppose you have a score panel consisting of marks of certain students (and their name).

```
val scorePanel = Map(
  ("Aaron", 75),
  ("Silvia", 90),
  ("Dan", 87),
  ("Clara", 62),
  ("Ron", 35)
)
```

Also consider the following grading system. Below 40 marks is not passed. Thereafter less than 65 is 'lower division'. Thereafter less than 80 is 'first division' and 80 or above is 'distinction'

Based on how well someone has scored, they are eligible for certain type of subjects. For instance only pass are eligible for single credit math. First division can get double credit math with chemistry, and a distinction is eligible for triple credit math with physics and chemistry.

...

Getting the score from the scorePanel should yield an Option. Because the scorePanel may not have marks for a given name. [e.g. if you are looking for marks of 'Rivan', it should return None. This is a case of (otherwise) null handling]

def getScore(name: String): Option[Int] = scorePanel.get(name)

Eligibility can be modelled as a trait with three variations.

trait Eligibility

case object SingleCreditMathOnly extends Eligibility

case object DoubleCreditMathAndChemistry extends Eligibility

case object TripleCreditMathPhysicsChemistry extends Eligibility

Given the marks, we can model grading the Option way like this -

def grading(marks: Int): Option[String] = {

if (marks < 40) None

else if (marks < 65) Some("lower division")

else if (marks < 80) Some("first division")

else Some("distinction")

}

This is better because failed score does not need to be

considered for processing for Eligibility. Note that Eligibility for grading is determined the following way -

```
def elig(gradeDesc:String): Eligibility = gradeDesc match {
  case "lower division" => SingleCreditMathOnly
  case "first division" => DoubleCreditMathAndChemistry
  case "distinction" => TripleCreditMathPhysicsChemistry
}
```

If we returned a String like 'failed' from grading (instead of Option), and that String would be directly passed to the *elig* function, it would not be able to return a valid Eligibility object against it. Wrapping only valid divisions in Some, in the grading method, it is ensured that *elig* function would need to consider only valid grades to work on.

...

At this stage, given a name (whether it is existing in the scorePanel or not [and that is a point in processing with possible data exception]) the eligibility can be checked as follows -

```
def checkElig(name: String): Option[Eligibility] = getScore(name) flatMap (grading) map (elig)
```

It takes care of, whether the score is available for the name, and whether he has had a valid division for any form of eligibility.

The same can also happen with a for comprehension.

```
def checkElig(name: String) = for {
  marksOpt <- getScore(name)
  elg <- grading(marksOpt)
} yield (elg)
```

Here too (like Lists) the innermost level of generator should use map and all other levels have to use flatMap.

The whole solution is given below.

```
object Optfor {


  val scorePanel = Map(
    ("Aaron", 75),
    ("Silvia", 90),
    ("Dan", 87),
    ("Clara", 62),
    ("Ron", 35)
  )


  def main(args: Array[String]) = {
  println("Rivan => " + checkElig("Rivan"))
  println("Ron => " + checkElig("Ron"))
  println("Clara => " + checkElig("Clara"))
  println("Silvia => " + checkElig("Silvia"))
  }


  def getScore(name: String): Option[Int] = scorePanel.get(name)


  def grading(marks: Int): Option[String] = {
    if (marks < 40) None
    else if (marks < 65) Some("lower division")
```

```scala
    else if (marks < 80)  Some("first division")
    else  Some("distinction")
}


trait Eligibility
case object SingleCreditMathOnly extends Eligibility
case object DoubleCreditMathAndChemistry extends Eligibility
case object TripleCreditMathPhysicsChemistry extends Eligibility


def elig(gradeDesc:String): Eligibility = gradeDesc match {
  case "lower division" => SingleCreditMathOnly
  case "first division" => DoubleCreditMathAndChemistry
  case "distinction" => TripleCreditMathPhysicsChemistry
}


//works :
//def checkElig(name: String): Option[Eligibility] =
getScore(name) flatMap (grading) map (elig)
//works :
//def checkElig(name: String): Option[Eligibility] =
getScore(name) flatMap (marksOpt => grading(marksOpt) map
elig)


//works :
def checkElig(name: String) = for {
```

marksOpt <- getScore(name)

   elg <- grading(marksOpt)

  } yield (elg)

}

Optfor.main(Array())

    Which produces -

Rivan => None

Ron => None

Clara => Some(lower division)

Silvia => Some(distinction)

'Optionifying' functions

    In order to incorporate exception handling using Options, it is not necessary to start rewriting the entire code base (to change functions to take and return Options instead of other type that they were doing). There is an easy way to convert a normal (unary) function A => B to a function of type *Option[A] => Option[B]* using *map*.

def lift[A,B](f: A => B): Option[A] => Option[B] = _ map f

    For example -

scala> def lift[A,B](f: A => B): Option[A] => Option[B] = _ map f

lift: [A, B](f: A => B)Option[A] => Option[B]

scala> def howlong: String => Int = (str:String) => str.length howlong: String => Int

scala> def liftedLength = lift(howlong)

liftedLength: Option[String] => Option[Int]

In a slightly different manner, for a binary function such as - f: (A, B) => C

A function may be implemented, that takes Options of the input type, and using this function internally, produces Option of the output type.

def map2[A,B,C](a: Option[A], b: Option[B])(f: (A, B) => C): Option[C]

The implementation is rather trivial through pattern matching.

def map2[A,B,C](a: Option[A], b: Option[B])(f: (A, B) => C): Option[C] = (a,b) match {

case (Some(a), Some(b)) => Some(f(a,b))

case _ => None

}

Note that it is meaningless to invoke the function *f* unless both the options have useful values. Hence all cases other than (Some(a), Some(b)) should return None.

List and Option

In many transformational pipeline, both List(s) and Option(s) may occur. A few quick tips, for such cases, may be useful.

Flattening List of Options
Firstly flattening a List of Options, results in a List

consisting of inner elements of the Lists Option which are not None, and Nones are discarded.

scala> val l = List(Some(1), None, Some(2), None)

l: List[Option[Int]] = List(Some(1), None, Some(2), None)

scala> l.flatten

reso: List[Int] = List(1, 2)

This could prove to be a quick way of gathering useful values in many situations.

Sequence
Secondly a function may be implemented (and such function or equivalent may exist in prominent FP APIs) which converts a List of Options (of some type) to an Option of List of the same type.

def sequence[A](l: List[Option[A]]): Option[List[A]]

Note that since the Output is an Option type (Option of List[A]), it encapsulates an element of uncertainty. If you were guaranteed to get back a List[A], even an empty one, there wouldn't be much point in wrapping it in Option (it could be just List[A] instead). The uncertainty part comes in because if any of the Option in the original List turns out to be None, then the return is None. Otherwise it hands over the full List of inner elements wrapped in Some.

(Contrast that with flatten of List of Options discussed earlier.)

What could be the use case? In order to use a more non programmatic analogy - say you want to cook a delicate dish, for which you need 12 ingredients. You send your friend to the shop, and he comes back with 11 ingredients. Is this going to be of use to you? (note the word 'delicate'). So in certain cases, you may be interested in the result, only if it's available in it's entirety. Otherwise it is of no use to you. Hope I could make the point.

How could you implement such a function. The following should work -

def sequence[A](l: List[Option[A]]): Option[List[A]] =

l.foldRight(Some(Nil: List[A]):Option[List[A]])((oa, ola) => oa.flatMap(a => ola.map(la => a :: la)))

What is happening here?

Note that the foldRight is being called on List (and not on Option), foldRight is being used to build the final list ground up (or starting from the right), and hence starting with the empty List (Nil) of appropriate type as the initial value (z) of fold.

Since it is a foldRight (folding starting from right) the compact element (final type) will always be the right argument of the fold operation. Hence, of the (oa, ola) - oa represents each individual option elements from the List in turn and, ola is the compacted Option.

Now the fold operation itself consists of a series of operations. In the first stage, flatMap is being called on the Option element. [Note that both map and flatMap brings out the inner element of a structure, to do operation on that]. The flatMap brings out the inner element of the Option (represented by a), and then uses it's inner function which is a => ola.map(la => a :: la) The type of the function should be A => Option[List[A]] (because we are 'flatmapping' on type Option[A] and we expect it to provide Option[List[A]]. Since the output type of inner function of flatMap and the output type of the flatMap itself should be same, hence the inner function output type should be Option[List[A]])

[Note also that although ola is not part of the argument

of the inner function of flatMap, it is still available in context as it is an argument for an outer function]

So for the inner function of flatMap, which should be of type A => Option[List[A]], we got the *a* (of correct type), but is the output type correct? i.e. is ola.map(la => a :: la) of type Option[List[A]] ?

Note that *ola* itself is the final type Option[List[A]]. mapping on that will bring out the inner type of the option, and hence la should be of type List[A]. Also map on option will produce an Option. inner type of which would be the result type of map's inner function i.e. the type of *a :: la* But *a :: la* is prepending an A onto a List[A] so the result is of type List[A]. So output of the map would be of type Option[List[A]]

The solution type checks.

The fold operation can be type noted as -

(Option[A], Option[List[A]]) => <Option[A]>.flatMap(A => <Option[List[A]]>.map(List[A] => List[A]))

For a simple demonstration of the working of the function -

scala> val l1 = List(Some(1), None, Some(2))

l1: List[Option[Int]] = List(Some(1), None, Some(2))

scala> val l2 = List(Some(1), Some(2), Some(3))

l2: List[Some[Int]] = List(Some(1), Some(2), Some(3))

scala> sequence(l1)

res2: Option[List[Int]] = None

scala> sequence(l2)

res3: Option[List[Int]] = Some(List(1, 2, 3))

example – ingredients and recipes

For a more fitting (?) example of sequence, suppose you know certain recipe to cook a few things. What ingredients each of those dishes require is given by -

val recipes = Map(

  "Cupcake" -> List("Flour", "Sugar", "Egg", "Butter"),

  "Omlette" -> List("Egg", "Onion", "Chili", "Salt"),

  "Sandwich" -> List("Bread", "Egg", "Sauce", "Lettuce")

)

And what your pantry has is given by -

val pantry = List(

  "Egg",

  "Flour",

  "Butter",

  "Onion",

  "Bread",

  "Chili",

  "Salt",

  "Oil"

) map (s => (s, s)) toMap

Now you need to enquire whether you have all ingredients for a particular dish. Note that if even a single ingredient is missing, that would mean you can not make the dish (and hence you might as well have none!). Hence this is a classic case for using the sequence function. This could be used to check the availability of ingredients for a particular dish as follows -

def canMake(dish: String): Boolean =

recipes.get(dish).map(_.map(pantry.get(_))).map(sequence(_)).fla tten.map(_ => true).getOrElse(false)

In the way of explanation -

recipes.get(dish) will produce an Option with a List of ingredients (Strings) *wrapped in Some*, for a valid dish, or *None* if an invalid dish was enquired. The first *map* on that - gets the List inside (for valid recipes), and the second *map* is on that *List (of Strings)*. The mapping on ingredients List looks through the pantry for each required ingredients, and produces an ingredient (String) wrapped in Some or None (for each one of them), and hence it finally produces a list of Options. The outer map (first map) makes it an Option (of List of Options) so another map is needed to get out the List of Options form that Option of List of Options. Which is then passed through the sequence function to produce an Option of List (either a List of ingredients wrapped in Some if all ingredients are available, or None). But the sequence itself is occurring within a map of Option. So the overall result of the map will be Option of Option of List, and hence a flatten is needed to reduce one level of optioning to an Option of List. A *map* on that, is simply checking if a List exists (which means all ingredients are available) in which case it returns true. Otherwise, if a list does not exist inside the option, it may either mean, the name of the dish was invalid so None was available from recipes Map, or that all the ingredients were not available in the pantry. In either case it is a false. The dish is not possible to be prepared.

...

The whole solution is given below -

```scala
import scala.language.postfixOps

object Dish {

  val recipes = Map(
    "Cupcake" -> List("Flour", "Sugar", "Egg", "Butter"),
    "Omlette" -> List("Egg", "Onion", "Chili", "Salt"),
    "Sandwich" -> List("Bread", "Egg", "Sauce", "Lettuce")
  )

  val pantry = List(
    "Egg",
    "Flour",
    "Butter",
    "Onion",
    "Bread",
    "Chili",
    "Salt",
    "Oil"
  ) map (s => (s, s)) toMap
```

```scala
def sequence[A](l: List[Option[A]]): Option[List[A]] =
  l.foldRight(Some(Nil: List[A]):Option[List[A]])((oa, ola) =>
    oa.flatMap(a => ola.map(la => a :: la)))


def canMake(dish: String): Boolean =

  recipes.get(dish).map(_.map(pantry.get(_))).map(sequence(_)).fla
tten.map(_ => true).getOrElse(false)


def main(args: Array[String]) = {
  println("Ingerdients available for Omlette1 : " +
canMake("Omlette1"))

  println("Ingerdients available for Cupcake : " +
canMake("Cupcake"))

  println("Ingerdients available for Omlette : " +
canMake("Omlette"))

}

}


Dish.main(Array())
```

Which produces -

Ingerdients available for Omlette1 : false

Ingerdients available for Cupcake : false

Ingerdients available for Omlette : true

example – bonus report

One final example demonstrating the use of map, flatMap and filter on Options.

Suppose you have employee records mapped with employee ids.

```
val empRecords = Map(

 3 -> EmpRec(3, "Aaron", "Permanent", "trainee", 30000.00),

 4 -> EmpRec(4, "Silvia", "Permanent", "manager", 120000.00),

 5 -> EmpRec(5, "Dan", "Permanent", "developer", 90000.00),

 7 -> EmpRec(7, "Clara", "Permanent", "seniorManager", 150000.00),

 6 -> EmpRec(6, "Ron", "Casual", "developer", 65000.00)
)
```

The task is to get the Bonus report of an employee, given his id.

But there are few extra cases to be considered. Firstly the record for the given id may not exist in the Map. Secondly if he is a Casual employee, he is not considered for bonus. For any other employees, bonus is declared only for developer (5%), manager(10%) and seniorManager (20%). The report should indicate "No bonus" for any invalid case, and provide a report of bonus in the form *Bonus for <name> [id=<id>] = <bonus up to 2 decimal>*

(e.g. Bonus for Dan [id=5] = 4500.00)

Solution :

You can think about the solution in pieces, and then try

to put the pieces together. (Considering a consistent solution exists, this should be quiet possible in functional programming way)

...

Clearly the input records could be modelled with -

case class EmpRec(id:Int, name: String, typ:String, desig:String, salary:Double)

and for output records. notice that the actual data required are *employee name, id* and *bonus amount*. So it could be modelled with a case class -

case class Rpt(id:Int, name: String, bonus:Double)

But since we need to format the output in a certain way, we can override the toString method of the case class.

case class Rpt(id:Int, name: String, bonus:Double) {

override def toString() =

"Bonus for " + name + " [id=" + id + "] = " + "%.02f".format(bonus)

}

...

The getting of a record from the *empRecords* Map can be expressed with -

def getEmp(id:Int): Option[EmpRec] = empRecords.get(id)

And checking if an employee is Casual could be -

def isCasual(emp: EmpRec): Boolean = emp.typ == "Casual"

...

Given the salary and percentage of bonus, the actual bonus can be calculated simply with -

*def calcBonus(salary: Double, pct: Int): Double = (salary * pct) / 100.00*

And for the Permanent employees, the bonus percentage where applicable, can be expressed through a function -

def bonusDec(emp: EmpRec): Option[Int] = emp.desig match {

  case "developer" => Some(5) //percent

  case "manager" => Some(10)

  case "seniorManager" => Some(20)

  case _ => None //includes trainee

}

   ...

While putting the pieces together, to get to the final solution, note that given the pieces are valid, how they will be put together may be dictated by the pieces themselves.

Clearly *isCasual* is a predicate and fit to filter with, while *bonusDec* is a function taking a non Option and producing an Option (and hence a strong candidate for flatMapping with). With this reasoning we can start the assembly like -

getEmp(id)

.filter(!isCasual(_))

.flatMap(rec =>

  bonusDec(rec)

There will be more to come. But already a few things to be considered. Firstly why bonusDec produces an Option?

Note that the other way would have been outputting o

(zero) as bonus for invalid cases. However the function that processes the bonus percentage down the line might not always be capable of handling zero (and may be designed only to handle valid cases [Like a trait with valid possibilities only]. Not an ideal design perhaps, but still a possibility, if different parts of the functionality is designed / developed by different people). Hence outputting Option builds up a more solid foundation for the capacity to handle valid case only (and discard the rest using Option level API functions).

Secondly note that between *filter* and *flatMap*, not only *filter* handles binary case (yes/no), while *flatMap* is capable of handing more than two cases, *flatMap* can also add additional processing, while *filter* can not.

Note also that the *filter* is necessary here because if the Casual record (of Ron) is passed to the *bonusDec*, the outcome would be developer's percentage (because even though his position is Casual, his designation is developer).

...

After passing through *bonesDec*, we have an Optional percentage (Int) of bonus, but we still need the actual salary to calculate the bonus amount. And that is where binding a map inside the flatMap body comes handy (because inside the body, arguments available to the outer function is still in scope)

```
def rptBonus(id:Int): Option[Rpt] =

 getEmp(id)

 .filter(!isCasual(_))

 .flatMap( rec =>

  bonusDec(rec)

  .map(pct => calcBonus(rec.salary,pct))
```

```
  .map(bonus => Rpt(rec.id, rec.name, bonus))
)
```

Hence *calcBonus* can access the *pct* calculated by the *bonusDec* as well as the *salary*, which is part of *rec* (the original argument of the flatMapping function)

The final solution is of the shape -

```
object Demo {


  case class EmpRec(id:Int, name: String, typ:String, desig:String,
  salary:Double)
  case class Rpt(id:Int, name: String, bonus:Double) {
    override def toString() =
      "Bonus for " + name + " [id=" + id + "] = " +
  "%.02f".format(bonus)

  }


  val empRecords = Map(
    3 -> EmpRec(3, "Aaron", "Permanent", "trainee", 30000.00),
    4 -> EmpRec(4, "Silvia", "Permanent", "manager", 120000.00),
    5 -> EmpRec(5, "Dan", "Permanent", "developer", 90000.00),
    7 -> EmpRec(7, "Clara", "Permanent", "seniorManager",
  150000.00),
    6 -> EmpRec(6, "Ron", "Casual", "developer", 65000.00)
  )


  def getEmp(id:Int): Option[EmpRec] = empRecords.get(id)
```

```
//for filtering - binary choice
def isCasual(emp: EmpRec): Boolean = emp.typ == "Casual"


//for mapping
def calcBonus(salary: Double, pct: Int): Double = (salary * pct) /
100.00


//for flatMapping
def bonusDec(emp: EmpRec): Option[Int] = emp.desig match {
  case "developer" => Some(5) //percent
  case "manager" => Some(10)
  case "seniorManager" => Some(20)
  case _ => None //includes trainee
}


def rptBonus(id:Int): Option[Rpt] =
  getEmp(id)
  .filter(!isCasual(_))
  .flatMap( rec =>
    bonusDec(rec)
    .map(pct => calcBonus(rec.salary,pct))
    .map(bonus => Rpt(rec.id, rec.name, bonus))
  )
```

```scala
def main(args: Array[String]) = {

    println("employee [id = 1] : " + rptBonus(1).getOrElse("No
bonus"))

    println("employee [id = 3] : " + rptBonus(3).getOrElse("No
bonus"))

    println("employee [id = 4] : " + rptBonus(4).getOrElse("No
bonus"))

    println("Declared bonuses : ")

    empRecords.keys.toList.map(id =>
rptBonus(id)).flatten.foreach(println)

  }


}


Demo.main(Array())
```

And it demonstrates handling of cases for 'valid bonus' and 'valid employee with no bonus', as well as 'invalid employee id' case.

When run, this should produce -

employee [id = 1] : No bonus

employee [id = 3] : No bonus

employee [id = 4] : Bonus for Silvia [id=4] = 12000.00

Declared bonuses :

Bonus for Dan [id=5] = 4500.00

Bonus for Clara [id=7] = 30000.00

Bonus for Silvia [id=4] = 12000.00

...

This is where our present journey of exception handling comes to an end. Note that Options are by no means the only structure available for exception handling (and you may continue to explore other options including *Either*), but this gives a good way of handling invalid cases without getting into null values.